REDISCOVER BRITISH CRAFTSMANSHIP

TOM QUINN

David and Charles

A DAVID & CHARLES BOOK
Copyright © David & Charles Ltd, 2010

David & Charles is an F+W Media, Inc. Company
4700 East Galbraith Road Cincinnati, OH 45236

First published in the UK in 2010

Text © David & Charles Ltd, 2010
Images © see page 256
Mastercrafts television programme, format and title graphics
© Ricochet

BBC and the BBC logo are trademarks of the British
Broadcasting Corporation and are used under licence.
BBC logo © BBC 1996

Tom Quinn has asserted his right to be identified as author
of this work in accordance with the Copyright, Designs and
Patents Act, 1988.

A catalogue record for this book is available from
the British Library.

ISBN 13: 978-0-7153-3643-4
ISBN 10: 0-7153-3643-6

Printed in the UK by Butler Tanner & Dennis Ltd, Frome
For David & Charles Ltd
Brunel House, Newton Abbot, Devon, TQ12 4PU

Publisher: Stephen Bateman
Commissioning Editor: Neil Baber
Editorial Manager: Emily Pitcher
Editor: Verity Muir
Art Editor: Prudence Rogers
Design Manager: Sarah Clark
Project Editor: Val Porter
Production: Bev Richardson, Jodie Culpin
Photographers: Lorna Yabsley, Paul Felix

www.davidandcharles.co.uk

Contents

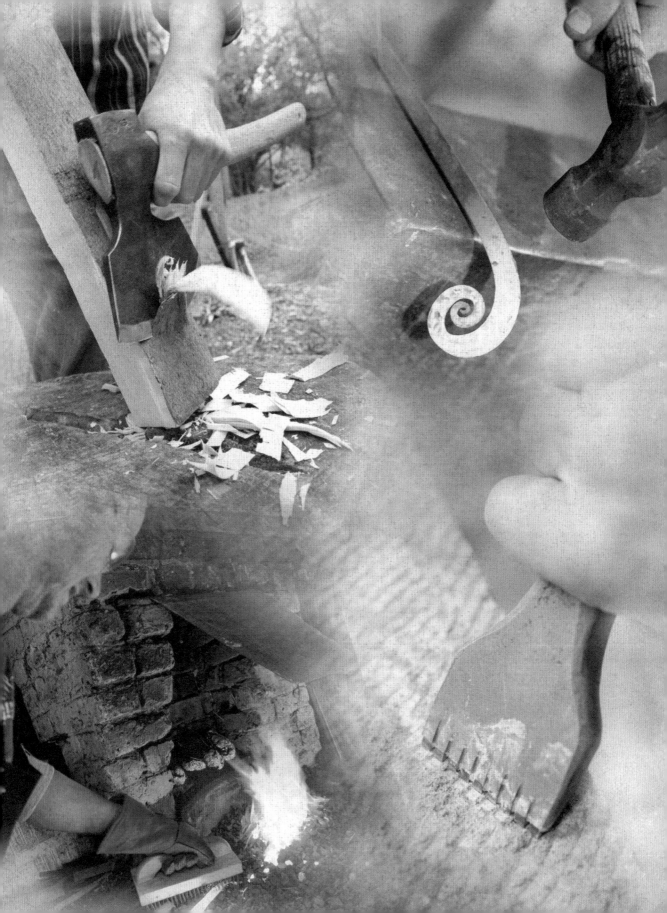

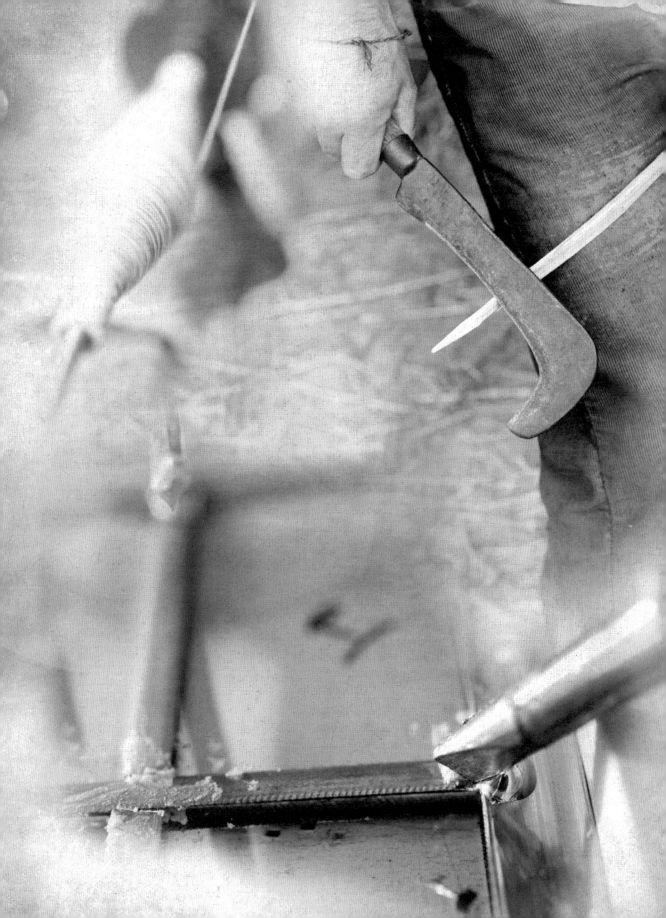

Introduction

'What makes a person happy,' wrote John Seymour a quarter of a century ago, 'is doing work that he or she loves, being fairly paid for it, and having it properly appreciated.' He was writing about the 'forgotten arts' of traditional woodland crafts, building crafts, workshop crafts, textile crafts and more; crafts that, ever since so many of them became mechanised and absorbed into factories, have been said to be dying or already extinct. But they were wrong! Those traditional crafts, producing artefacts that are original, personal and very much not mass produced, continue to be practised in homes and workshops in hidden corners all over Britain. And there are many of us who, if only we had the time, training and skill, would love to master those crafts ourselves.

For the BBC television series *Mastercrafts*, the lucky few were given that opportunity: they were taught by masters in a range of crafts and a range of raw materials – wood, metal, straw, glass, stone and fibre – and were encouraged to express the creativity that is in the nature of human beings. The luckiest will continue to learn and practise their new craft, and might even succeed in being 'fairly paid' for their creations by the growing number of people who, while appreciating the low price of mass-produced

{ *These traditional crafts continue to be practised in homes and workshops* }

goods, yearn for something more: something that has absorbed the spirit and personality of its maker, something that connects with the origins of its material, something real. When you look at the objects in your home, for how many of them do you know their history – who designed them, whose hands made them (and where and how), where the tree was grown that provided the wood, where the stone was quarried, or from what breed of sheep the wool was shorn and on which farm? There is so much more to an object than its utility. There should be a story in each one.

This book looks at some of the crafts in several dimensions, starting with the raw materials. What are they and where do they come from? How do you find the right stone, the ore from which you can smelt a metal? What is glass made from? How is flax turned into threads that can be woven into linen? What else can be made out of the raw material?

The practicalities of the crafts are explained – how to weave, how to forge iron, or blow glass, or thatch a roof, or turn wood on a pole lathe, or carve a block of marble – and the tools are described, to give you a working knowledge of the basics. Just as important is the tradition of the craft: when it was first practised thousands of years ago in different parts of the world, what evidence remains of those ancient skills, major developments in techniques over the centuries and where you can see examples representing those developments.

Each chapter has an interview with a master craftsman or woman, and each chapter seeks to inspire more to join their ranks. It is far from easy to become skilled, especially now that the old system of apprenticeships and guilds has all but vanished, and it is certainly not easy to market what has been lovingly handmade. But for those who have an innate ability and who persist and believe in their work, the rewards are far, far richer than being 'fairly paid'. They lie in the satisfaction of creating something beautiful, unique and lasting that will become part of our heritage – something that future generations will admire and perhaps be inspired by to continue the craft tradition themselves.

> *There is so much more to an object than its utility. There should be a story in each one*

STONEWORK

The Craft of Stonework

Stone is more difficult, expensive and unforgiving to work with than plant matter such as wood and thatch, and requires more robust tools. There is less margin for making mistakes when working with stone: once a piece has been chipped off in error, the damage has been done. Like a woodworker, a stoneworker needs to understand the character of each piece of stone and choose the raw material wisely.

The vernacular use of local building stone gives a strong identity to many parts of Britain: you know at once that you are in the Cotswolds when the villages are built of honey-coloured limestone, or that you are in Cornwall when you see granite cottages with slate roofs. The pale grey limestone buildings with Collyweston split-stone roofs immediately give a sense of place in Northamptonshire; grey sandstone reminds you that you are in Dales country; and so on for different regions where local stone is at the very heart of the landscape.

The British Geological Survey reckons that more than one thousand different types of decorative and building stone have been quarried and used at some time in Britain. Adding the worldwide figure to that, the

> *More than one thousand different types of decorative and building stone have been quarried and used at some time in Britain*

number of types of stone used for building and carving can be multiplied many times.

Stone can be classified into three basic groups: metamorphic, igneous and sedimentary.

Durable granite

Granite is probably the best known of all the igneous rocks, which are typically very hard and crystalline. Igneous rocks were formed as molten magma cooled under enormous pressure deep under the earth's crust. Looked at closely, granite reveals large crystals of quartz as well as what are known

as feldspars (pink and white areas of the stone), and black ferromagnesian minerals such as mica. The sizes of these various elements produce different types of granite, from Kashmir white through pinks and reds to Volga blue.

Granite is found in pockets in Britain, such as in southwest England and in Scotland. Through most of the industrial revolution – certainly from the early nineteenth century until the end of the twentieth – Britain was the world's biggest producer of granite, with major quarries around Aberdeen and Peterhead in Scotland exporting to the rest of the world. Granite quarries in Devon and Cornwall also supplied a seemingly insatiable demand for this durable of building stones.

Sandstones and limestones

The most widely used and geologically most widespread building stones in Britain are not igneous but sedimentary. Sedimentary rocks are grouped as clastic (made up of broken pieces of older rocks), organic

ABOVE *Limestone is quarried largely from a great S-shaped belt of rocks stretching from Dorset through the Cotswolds to Lincolnshire and Yorkshire.*

LEFT *Granite is hard to cut but has few flaws, and it can be ground and polished. 'The Cheesewring', so named because of its resemblance to a stack of cheese, can be found at the top of Stowe's Hill in Cornwall.*

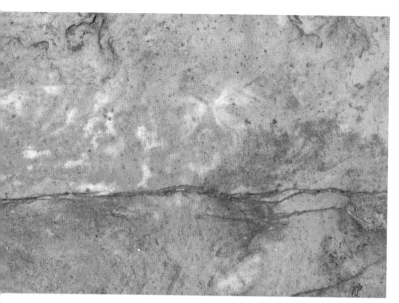

TOP *Sandstone varies in colour, the most common being brown, pink, red and cream; Yorkshire sandstone is brown and blue.*

ABOVE *Wells Cathedral in Somerset was built in the twelfth century using Doulting stone. The grey columns on the west front are Kilkenny marble, a fine-grained limestone from Ireland. The Jurassic Great oolite limestone, better known as Bath stone, was used for fine carved work, such as the font.*

(based on what was once living matter) and chemical precipitates. The most typical sedimentary building stones are limestones and sandstones.

When all of Britain's building-stone quarries, both historic and current, are plotted on a map, a useful line can be drawn from Scarborough in Yorkshire to Exeter in Devon. To the north and west of that line the bulk of the stones that have been quarried are sandstones while to the east they are predominantly limestones, though there are patches of each on the other side of this imaginary line.

Sandstones are clastic: they are made up of tiny sand-grains of feldspar and quartz, and sometimes other rock minerals, all held together by calcite (calcium carbonate), silica or other cementing minerals. A high quartz content makes sandstone an excellent and relatively hardwearing building material that is also fairly easy to work – at least compared with granite.

Limestones are organically based: they are composed mostly of calcite derived from minute marine creatures compressed over millions of years. Limestones have been quarried from local outcrops up and down the country for everything from large manor houses to tiny cottages and farm buildings, but they also achieved international recognition via exports from huge quarries for oolithic limestones at Portland in Dorset and at Combe Down in Somerset, the home of Bath stone. It is these oolithic limestones (so called because they comprise 'egg-shaped' grains) that are of most interest since they have been used for centuries to construct some of Britain's most loved and best known buildings and churches.

The list of limestone buildings in Britain reveals this stone's central role in the history of architecture: Portland stone for St Paul's Cathedral; chalky clunch for the interior of

Ely Cathedral; sand-coloured Anston stone from Yorkshire for the Houses of Parliament; Doulting stone from the Mendips for Wells Cathedral; and magnesian limestone for York Minster. Limestone was ideal for these highly decorated buildings because it is relatively soft and therefore easily carved.

There are many different limestones; most of the South Downs, for example, is composed of fine-grained chalk limestone. An important group is the magnesian limestones or dolomites from areas such as Mansfield and Tadcaster. Purbeck marble from Dorset, another of Britain's best-known stones, is not actually marble at all – it's a polished limestone that has been used since Roman times. Smaller quarries around the country yielded other specialist limestones, including Hopton Wood in Derbyshire, which was famous for producing limestone for paving stones, carved fireplaces and those sad and seemingly endless rows of stone crosses seen in the First World War cemeteries of Northern France.

Marble and slate

The final group is the metamorphic rocks, formed by intense heat and pressure, and they have a crystalline structure but also sedimentary elements.

Marble – a metamorphosed limestone is probably the most famous in this group. It is a hard stone but relatively easy to carve. The world's best-known marble is produced in Italy at Carrara but small amounts of marble have been quarried in Britain in the past – from the Islands of Skye and Iona, for example.

For building material the most important of all native metamorphic rocks in Britain is slate for roofing, typically quarried in Cumbria and Wales. Slate originated from sedimentary shale rocks based on clay or volcanic ash, and is mostly quartz and mica.

Limestone is ideal for highly decorated buildings because it is relatively soft and therefore easily carved

Stone on the move

Despite a wealth of native quarries, much stone has been imported to Britain for specialist work. Black marble from Tournai in Belgium, for example, has been imported since medieval times. It was famously used to make Cardinal Wolsey's sarcophagus in 1524, but when Wolsey died in disgrace it

was kept in store for three centuries and then used for Nelson! Today marble and granite – not to mention sandstones and limestones – can be bought from quarries across the world, and in an astonishing array of colours from green and blue to red, white, yellow and black, and delivery can be expected in some cases within days. American architects now routinely order marble from Italy, and in the City of London recent buildings have made use of stone from India and Australia.

A big problem with stone in earlier times was the cost and difficulty of transportation even within Britain. Local stone really did mean local, because to move bulk quantities just a few miles was a major undertaking. However, the development of Britain's canal system in the eighteenth century changed this completely and stone began to be moved relatively cheaply to wherever it was needed. With the arrival of the railways stone could be moved both cheaply and quickly, which explains why Welsh roofing slate began to appear on houses in the most remote parts of the country and on buildings that had traditionally been roofed in thatch.

Today there is a move back towards using local stone, and Britain still boasts more than three hundred and fifty stone quarries, producing everything from world-famous Bath stone to specialist granites and sandstones.

STONE FROM THE GROUND

The simplest way of quarrying stone is to find a source of loose boulders, select the size you need, dig it up and cart it away. But when the boulders run out, the stone has to be quarried from the bedrock and each chosen block needs to be cut out from its surroundings.

Ancient stonemasons quickly realised a fundamental principle on which all attempts

to quarry, cut and shape stone are based: you can only cut stone if you are using a tool that is harder than the material you are cutting. The Egyptians – probably the best stoneworkers of the ancient world – were also the best metallurgists. They worked mainly in sandstone and limestone, but also used huge quantities of exceptionally hard granite, for which even their best copper and bronze tools were no match. The archaeological evidence suggests that their quarrying and cutting tools were made of dolerite, a dark green igneous stone even harder than granite.

When the size of the block to be quarried had been decided and marked out, teams of workers would begin to create a narrow trench all around the block by pounding the surrounding bedrock into powder with their dolerite balls, many of which have been found by archaeologists. Once the trench had been cut to the required depth, the quarrymen would undermine the block with a shallow inward cut at its base, and then used enormous wooden levers to break out the block.

It is difficult to estimate how long it would have taken to cut out a block in this way but it would certainly have been very slow work

ABOVE *Much of the red granite used for Ancient Egyptian temples and colossi came from quarries in Aswan. The Unfinished Obelisk of Aswan, shown here, still lies where it was abandoned after a crack was discovered as it was being extracted.*

LEFT *The sarcophagus of Lord Nelson lies beneath a complex arrangement of vaulted stonework in St Paul's cathedral.*

The modern stonemason's yard contains heavy machinery to transport the larger stone blocks and do the basic cutting work in preparation for the finer carving to be done by hand. The saw uses diamond-imbedded tungsten teeth, and the blade is doused with water during cutting to keep it cool and to disperse the slurry. The prepared

ABOVE *The elaborate mouldings of the main arches, the lavish use of polished Purbeck marble for the columns and the overall sculptural decoration of London's Westminster Abbey make it a unique example of fine stonework.*

{ *Beer stone was used in the building of more than a score of Britain's best known cathedrals* }

and very hard on the quarrymen. Many of the quarried blocks were massive; a block destined for an obelisk that remains in situ at a quarry in Aswan to this day would have been more than 40m (131ft) tall had it been cut out fully, but work came to a halt when a huge crack was discovered.

All quarrying techniques try to find the natural lines of weakness in the stone and exploit them in the process of removal. Today it is still common for blocks to be removed by cutting narrow trenches, just as the Egyptians did, but now using power rock drills and saws. Alternatively, what is known as percussive splitting (driving wedges into the stone) may be used. Blasting techniques, though quick, are only rarely used to extract stone from quarries: the problem with trying to extract stone too quickly is that it may be damaged in the process.

Right into the twentieth century stone-digging and quarrying in the traditional way used simple hand tools, strength and skill. The stone-digger located a block of stone in the pit, removed all the topsoil and dug around the block, wheeling the soil away in a barrow. In a sandstone pit, for example, he might unearth a stone weighing five or ten tons – the size of a room. Having dug all around it, he would inspect the stone to locate its weak points and cracks and then use metal wedges and a sledge hammer (weighing as much as 6–7kg (14–16lbs) or pick axe to split it into manageable hunks that could be levered out and loaded on a wagon for removal. Many stone-diggers were also skilled at cutting up stone into building blocks and 'facing' them, being paid by the cubic yard.

There is one rather special quarry at Beer, in East Devon, that offers a glimpse of two thousand and more years of quarrying by hand. Beer stone, a type of limestone, has been quarried from underground caverns here since Roman times. Relatively easy to carve and a beautiful smooth white in colour when it is exposed to the air, Beer stone was used in the building of more than a score of Britain's best known cathedrals. It was often chosen for delicate tracery work and was used extensively at Westminster Abbey, Hampton Court and Windsor Castle.

Roman chisel marks can still be seen on the cave walls at Beer, where the caves extend to more than seventy acres, all cut out by hand over two millennia. Old photographs and tools displayed in Beer Quarry Caves show that, even at the end of the nineteenth century, blocks were still cut out by hand and then the blocks, each weighing at least 4,064kg (4tons), were winched on to wagons for removal by teams of horses, often to load the stone on to barges at the nearby beach for transportation to destinations that might be hundreds of miles away.

WORKING THE STONE

Building masons

Stonemasons who work in the building industry can be roughly divided into hewers, banker masons and fixers or setters. The hewer is the quarryman who gets the stone out of the ground. The banker mason cuts and carves stone fresh from the quarry to the desired size and shape on a bench (banker) in the workshop or yard; he will also carve patterns if required, and finally 'dress' or finish the stone so that the surfaces are rough, smooth or polished, according to his brief. His work is then fixed in position at the building site by the fixer.

Banker masons traditionally attached marks for the fixer on each stone in places that wouldn't be seen once the building was complete. These marks, which can incorporate unique figures that identify the

mason, are fascinating when uncovered by later generations.

For building stone today, high-powered saws are used to cut blocks to size but detailing is still done by hand, and there is a precision about stone working that is still vital. When a stone arch is created or repaired, for example, it is built resting on a wooden formwork, but when that formwork is removed the arch will only stay up and remain load bearing (in the case of, say, a bridge) if it has been perfectly cut, with the keystone at the apex of the arch slotted precisely into position.

Stone carvers

Stone carving is a notoriously difficult skill to master. When one looks at the simple tools of the carver it is astonishing that magnificent works of art such as the front of Exeter Cathedral could be produced. But as with so

BELOW *Limestone and sandstone are the most familiar types of stone used for building. Many can be worked easily in any direction and are often called freestones. Both vary considerably in hardness and durability – some are almost as hard as granite while others can be cut with a simple handsaw.*

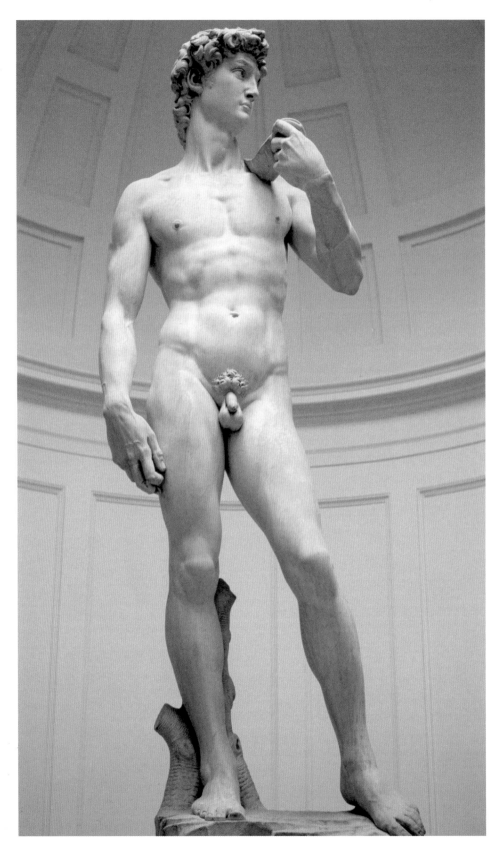

RIGHT *The marble chosen by Michelangelo for his famous sculpture, David, caused considerable difficulty in its restoration. While the cleaning removed decades of grimy build-up, better revealing the statue's iconic physique, it also highlighted the imperfect nature of the marble used to sculpt it.*

many things, it is not the tools that matter so much as the skill of the person using them.

It is a slow, delicate business – which is why the restoration of the front of Wells Cathedral in 1975, for example, took more than a decade. Whether working in marble, granite, basalt or sandstone, the process is the same. Very small amounts of stone are chipped or filed away while the block is positioned on a shock-absorbing material to prevent percussive damage by absorbing the hammer blows and restricting the effects of the chisel to the area being worked.

However confident the carver, the gradual process of carving in the round is immensely challenging. The figure or object being carved must look right from all angles and the least mistake – taking slightly too much stone away anywhere – cannot be reversed. Even a gargoyle, however hideous, wants to look its best.

Some of the difficulties that apply to all stone carving, but particularly marble, can be seen with Michelangelo's David – arguably the most famous marble statue in the world. Michelangelo used a single massive block of Carrara marble to create his statue at a time when the usual method with large statues was to use one block for the torso and separate smaller blocks for the legs and arms. These would be joined together using holes with pegs pushed into them.

Smaller pieces of marble are more likely to reveal their faults. Using just one block, as Michelangelo did, is extremely risky because deep inside the marble there may be flaws that are not visible on the outside. Michelangelo took a huge gamble and got away with it. His block of marble would have started out at perhaps 7.6m (25ft) high, and his contemporaries would have assumed there was a real danger that after years of labour (the statue took three years to complete) a tiny flaw would ruin the whole

thing at the last minute. The sculptor clearly felt he knew better, but then he always claimed that he was simply releasing the figure from the stone – which is why it is believed that he did not even have roughed out his plans before starting work.

Carving lettering is perhaps even more delicate work. Modern techniques involving sandblasting or the use of high powered water jets are spurred by the master craftsmen who still cuts lettering by using the same hammers and chisels that would have been familiar to his Roman antecedents.

> *However confident the carver, the gradual process of carving in the round is immensely challenging*

THE STONE CARVER'S TOOLS

Chisels, picks, saws and files are the key tools used by stonemasons. For decorative stone work and carving the hand chisel is still by far the most important tool and modern chisels differ from their medieval and earlier counterparts only in terms of the quality of the steel used to make them.

Faced with a rough block of marble or granite, the carver first needs to take

BELOW *Carved lettering, whether incised into the surface or raised against a recessed background, calls not only for the ability to produce well-cut shapes, but also for a well-developed sense of proportion and spacing.*

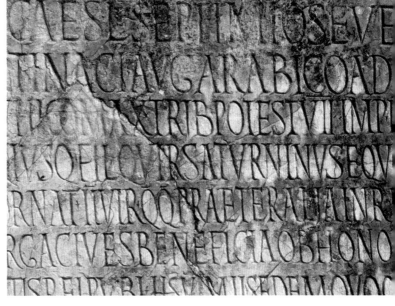

away relatively large areas of stone. Heavy pitching chisels are – as the name suggests – designed to do this. Once a rough shape begins to appear a narrow, solid metal tracing chisel is used to mark out lines to guide the carver. Point chisels come in a range of sizes and materials: hardened steel for use on softer stones, such as limestone, and carbide-tipped for use on very hard stones such as granite. Point chisels help to reduce the block further towards a stage where the finest work begins.

For centuries printers used stone as a medium from which to print

Toothed chisels are essentially smoothing tools and come in a range of sizes from, say, four-toothed for smaller areas to perhaps eight-toothed for larger areas. They allow smooth contours to be made and they remove the rough edges left by heavier pitching and point chisels. As with all chisels, the rule is the narrower the blade the more delicate the work.

Smoothers do exactly what the name suggests – they have rounded or fingernail-shaped blades of different sizes and are perfect for taking off just enough stone to leave an area with few rough marks. The fingernail-shaped chisel is known as a rondel or bullnose, and is used after the toothed chisel has created any rounded areas. Straight chisels are used to smooth areas left flat by the toothed chisel.

More specialised chisels include the cape or splitter, which is used to cut fine grooves in the stone. This curiously shaped tool is made with a narrow blade tip that widens out as you move up the blade towards the handle. For softer stone such as sandstone, a mason's gouge is used; this, like the similar woodworking tool, has a curved blade.

Stone polishing is a separate skill but the basic technique with marble, for example, is as follows. First of all, wet sandstone is rubbed on the surface of the marble. The surface is then rubbed using pieces of wet once-fired pottery or, for a very shiny finish, Gothland stone. For harder stones such as granite, the polishing process is similar, but emery (corundum) is also used as an abrasive. There is a theory that the ancient Egyptians used imported emery to work their granite.

BEYOND CONSTRUCTION

Apart from carving and building (which includes split roofing stone and slate as well as building blocks and stone flooring), stone has always had a great variety of uses. For example, sandstones from the stone area of 'Millstone Grit' of Derbyshire were traditionally dressed to make millstones for wind and water flour mills and smaller

BELOW *A wide variety of tools are used to handle and shape stone blocks and slabs into the final piece. The basic tools for shaping the stone are a mallet, chisels, and a metal straight edge.*

grindstones for the cutlery making industries of Sheffield; and large slabs of roughly cut stone in upland areas such as Cornwall, Devon and Yorkshire were used to make clapper bridges. For centuries printers used stone as a medium from which to print. The term 'lithography' literally means drawing on stone.

Slate, the cleaving of which is a craft in its own right, is not just a roofing material; it is used for floor tiles, inscribed gravestones and, in times gone by, for shove-ha'penny boards and billiard table tops as well as school blackboards and writing slates.

Then there are precious and semi-precious gemstones that are used in jewellery-making. This craft is heavily dependent on a wide range of stone types and the techniques for cleaving and cutting the stones recall, in many respects, the techniques of the stonemason. A cleaver may study a diamond for days, looking for lines of weakness that will enable him to cleave it with the minimum risk of shattering. With larger diamonds the process of cleaving, at least, is still carried out entirely by hand. Traditionally, gemstones such as topaz, emerald and ruby were cut and shaped by hand, but faceting machines are used today.

In contrast, a major use for stone over the millennia has been in road-making – everything from Roman slabs to cobblestones, flagstones and kerbstones (all of which required the services of a skilled stone cutter), and also crushed stones to make aggregate. Limestone is particularly useful: it is the source of cement, concrete and mortar in the road-making and building industries and is the basis of a wide range of other products from toothpaste to quicklime, poultry feed supplements and a soil dressing.

Stonemasonry and the working of stone has been at the heart of our culture for

thousands of years, providing the very symbols of civilisation in great buildings and sculptures, as well as countless practical items essential to our daily lives. But for fine examples of the stonemasons' art we need go no further than Britain's thousands of historic churchyards and cemeteries. For sheer variety of design and complexity, it's hard to beat the Highgate and Kensal Green cemeteries in London. Among a huge number of extraordinary funerary monuments, Kensal Green contains Greek temples, Egyptian halls, gothic fantasies and medieval castles, as well as the more ordinary – but equally fascinating – gravestones and tombs.

ABOVE *To construct a clapper bridge, one or more flat slabs of stone must rest upon stone piers set at intervals across a river. Originating from the Anglo-Saxon term 'clapper', meaning to bridge stepping stones, the design is believed to be prehistoric in origin, although most surviving examples date to the medieval period.*

Creating a flat surface is the basis of all architectural stonemasonry, and the first task an apprentice must master. Taking four measured points on the block the mason cuts in a small ledge and places 'boning blocks' on each; a ruler placed from one block to another quickly establishes where the block deviates from square, and

The Mastercrafter

ANDY
OLDFIELD

mixes the ongoing work of maintaining the stonework at Hardwick Hall in Derbyshire with private commissions for decorative carving.

'I love old buildings,' says stonemason Andy Oldfield, who works for the National Trust at one of Britain's most spectacular Elizabethan houses, Hardwick Hall in Derbyshire.

'I was taught the skills of the stonemason by Hardwick's master mason Trevor Hardy, and I'm now what's called the leading hand – I'm second in command as it were to Trevor. Working at Hardwick is a challenge and a privilege because the work we do repairing and conserving the stone will last for generations.'

After what he describes as something of a mid-life crisis, Andy retrained as a stonemason at the age of thirty-one. Before that he'd worked in a succession of different jobs – everything from factory hand to laser engineer. But nothing captured his imagination in the way that stone carving did.

'I loved it from the first day of my apprenticeship,' he says.

Like most apprenticeships the work of the stonemason starts with the basics, as Andy explains.

'It's quite simple really. You go to the quarry and get a rough block of stone. You then have to turn that rough block into a fairly precise cube. It's a process known as 'boning in'. You make a flat surface on one side of the stone, using a simple chisel and mallet combined with special wooden blocks that are effectively depth guides to stop you taking too much stone away and to ensure that your finished surface is level.'

Andy insists that the basis of his ancient craft is actually fairly straightforward. Once you are able to make a perfect cube – no easy task – you have all the basic skills necessary even for complex carving.

'Making that cube is the way you cut your teeth,' he says. 'There are four parts to the process. Pitching involves removing the first big areas of waste stone from the block. That's just the stone you don't want. Punching the waste off is the next stage – it's the same idea as pitching but you are taking off less stone. Next comes clawing the waste off – it's a finer technique for removing stone. Last and most delicate of all is chiselling the finish. Chiselling produces the end result.'

Once you have mastered these skills, says Andy, you can apply them to all architectural masonry work. Tools may differ in size for various jobs but the basics remain the same.

The stonemason's apprenticeship formerly lasted around seven years, but it is currently two to three years. Much of Andy's early training involved work on Hardwick Hall itself and Hardwick, as he explains, poses particular challenges:

'Hardwick is a sandstone house in an exposed position on a hill. Over the centuries – the hall was built in the 1590s – it's had a lot of wear and tear. We work continually

> *Once you are able to make a perfect cube you have all the basic skills necessary even for complex carving*

RIGHT *Any stone used for renovations on Hardwick Hall is quarried on site.*
BELOW *The serated-edged claw takes away waste stone in a more controllable way than a flat-edged chisel.*
FAR RIGHT *The 'ES' adorning the Hall are for Elizabeth Shrewsbury ('Bess of Hardwick'), the richest woman in Elizabethan England after the Queen herself.*

{ *We try to conserve wherever we can, which means using what is already there* }

on it, and we can spot immediately where good repairs have been done and where some not so good repairs have been done. We try to conserve wherever we can, which means using what is already there, but soft sandstone in an exposed position wears away quite quickly so we often have to take out worn sections of the stonework and replace them. Making a new piece to fit perfectly is very satisfying.' The stone to build the hall and its predecessor, the 'old hall', all came from the estate itself. Sandstone is still quarried there to this day, but only for the purpose of supplying Andy or his team with the means to keep the house in good repair.

Much of the work on the stone parts of the house centres on the strapwork around the turrets, the stone mullions and transoms of the windows (and there are a lot of windows), but the basic principle is that the

Sandstone is relatively
easy to work because it is
soft, whereas granite is
difficult because it is hard

ABOVE *A metal hammer creates a much sharper blow than softer mallets used for fine carving.*

BELOW *An apprentice's 'volute', one of the sculptural details of the Hall.*

house is repaired and conserved on a thirty-year cycle. 'That's how long to it takes to work right round the house and get back to where you started!'

Andy is also responsible for carefully recording the state of the stonework at the hall. 'We map, log, record and restore as we go.'

He is immensely proud of the long tradition of craftsmanship of which he is part. The materials from which the stonemason's tools are made may have changed here and there over the years, but in terms of their basic design, they would be instantly recognised by a medieval stonemason.

'Stonemasonry tool skills go back a thousand years and more,' he explains. 'In addition to the skills needed to work stone, there is the knowledge of stone itself. Different stones have very different qualities. Sandstone, for example, is relatively easy to work because it is soft, whereas granite is difficult because it is very hard.

'That's why granite chisels tend to be made in a far more resilient way,' says Andy. 'But for all stone, however hard or soft, you start by trying to remove a lot of stone, and work down through the layers to where you want to be.

'Once the stone is down to its basic shape the finer tools come into play. Decorative carving is difficult, there's no doubt about it.

We use fine tools and round nylon mallets – the heads of the mallets are round because it means they can be used from all angles. It's the same striking surface all round. Stonemason's mallets were once made from fruit wood, but nylon lasts much longer – perhaps as long as ten years.'

Away from his work at Hardwick Hall Andy accepts commissions for carvings. He's booked up for years ahead, and it's a part of the job he loves.

'I really enjoy figurative carving and I'm asked to do animals and people for all sorts of settings. I usually advise about the best kind of stone to use according to where it will be displayed – it might be a lovely tight-grained Portland stone for a commission that will be kept inside, but something completely different for an exposed, outdoor position.'

ABOVE *Andy's tools would be recognisable to the Elizabethan masons that worked on the site four centuries ago.*

A 'sinking square' and ruler are important pieces of the stonemason's toolkit. They are essential for achieving the flat surfaces and right angles, and checking that the block to be worked on is regular. Before embarking on mouldings or carvings, any pattern is carefully planned, marked out and templates created to lie on the surface.

The Tradition of Stonework

In regions where stone is readily accessible, the tradition of working it
has a very long history. And the nature of the material is such that a stone
monument or building can endure for thousands of years, so that the
history and development of stonemasonry and carving can be traced far
back into antiquity. Even small worked stone artefacts, such as prehistoric
flint tools, have a story to tell.

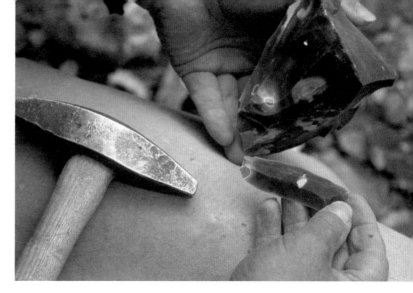

Stone has been used by man from the earliest times, and older than any other kind of stone working is flint knapping, a craft practised today by very few individuals in Britain. Flint is pure silicate, brittle and yet strong, it is not cut but 'knapped', by knocking or pushing flakes off it.

Grimes Caves in Norfolk show extensive stone workings where prehistoric peoples mined flints for thousands of years; these were then knapped into beautifully shaped axe and arrow heads. Examples of knapped flint tools and weapons can be seen in many museums, and the skill of the masons who worked the stone can be seen in the near-perfect symmetry of many of these artefacts, not to mention their superb cutting edges.

Flint could be worked with simple tools and, crucially, make useful objects. It could also be used to spark fire, and was still in use for this purpose in the seventeenth and eighteenth centuries to ignite the powder in flintlock guns. It has always been used as a building material, especially in regions where other stones are hard to find, and is still used today for building and also as a decorative material on the walls of churches, for example. The best quality flint in Britain comes from East Anglia, but there are rich pickings right across the South Downs through Sussex, Hampshire, Wiltshire and Dorset. Fist-sized spheres of flint might be built into lime-mortared walls (which is appropriate, as flint nodules are generally found in limestone beds and chalk), but with bigger pieces of flint the idea is to create one flat surface – that's the surface that would be seen in the wall – while the irregular shape of the rest of the flint would be used to lock each stone into another within the wall.

But the most famous of all ancient stonework comes from Egypt, where countless statues and monuments were produced with enormous skill by long-forgotten craftsmen during the Egyptian pre-dynastic and dynastic periods. The pyramids that remain are perhaps the most famous – and certainly the biggest – manmade stone edifices in the world. The great pyramid at Giza (which was built for the pharaoh Khufu, who ruled around 2575BCE) has a brick core but was originally clad in limestone, each slab cut to create a smooth uninterrupted surface. The pyramid is 146m (480ft) tall and extends to 228m (750ft) in each direction on the ground. Some of the most elaborate use of stone by the ancients took place in the old Middle Eastern Kingdoms. The world's museums are filled with countless smaller Egyptian stone carvings – from sphinxes, cats, gods and tutelary spirits to tiny scarab beetles and all in a wide range of stones from granite to lapis lazuli.

Carvings from the ancient civilisations of Mesopotamia (modern Iraq) include, for example, at least twenty stone figures of the Sumerian king Gudea. These are made in a range of stones, such as limestone and dolomite and, later, igneous

ABOVE *Flint with at least one straight face is known as knapped flint. Building with knapped flint is called flush work, and the flint would normally be knapped into cubes.*

LEFT *The twin temples at Abu Simbel in southern Egypt were carved out of the mountainside during the reign of Pharaoh Ramesses II in the thirteen century BCE. They took 20 years to build.*

{ *The most famous of all ancient stonework comes from Egypt* }

ABOVE *Roman use of stonework included ground engineering projects, like the Pont du Gard aqueduct in southern France. It is 274m (900ft) long and 49m (160ft) high, and originally delivered water to Nîmes (Nemausus).*

RIGHT *Easter Island, in the southeastern Pacific Ocean, is famous for the 887 monumental statues by the Stone Age Rapa Nui people.*

stones such as dolerite and diorite. Along with the remains of temples and many animal carvings, these date from around 2000BCE. Other Mesopotamian peoples, including the Babylonians (before 1600BCE) and the Assyrians (2400 to 612BCE), produced complex, highly sophisticated stone buildings and stone carvings. The palace of the Assyrian King Sargon II (721–705BCE), for example, was guarded by pairs of colossal human-headed winged bulls carved in stone. Two of these can be seen in the British Museum.

In ancient Europe the Greeks and Romans took methods of building with stone to new heights of sophistication and produced sculpture the equal of art of any age. There are magnificent examples of fine stonework right across the continent, from the Parthenon in Athens through the superb aqueduct of Pont du Gard in France, to the Pantheon and Coliseum in Rome. The stone-built city of Pompeii survives almost complete – here stone-lined streets can still be seen along with stone-walled houses, palaces and temples. Under the volcanic ash, archaeologists have uncovered numerous stone statues of the gods as well as stone

{ *Under the volcanic ash, archaeologists have uncovered numerous stone statues of the gods* }

gaming pieces, wells and cisterns, pillars and monuments.

On the other side of the world the Chinese, Japanese and Koreans had honed their stone-working skills long before the Christian era, producing superb statues of the Bhudda in a wide range of different stones. They also carved guardian figures for tombs and personal objects made of jade cut until the walls were so thin that they would allow light to pass through almost like glass. Among the most spectacular carvings of Buddha were the two giant sandstone figures 58 and 33m (190 and 108ft) high at Bamyan in Afghanistan, carved directly out of the cliffs in the sixth century and destroyed in 2002 by Muslim extremists.

In India an extremely ancient tradition of highly skilled stone-working produced, most famously the Taj Mahal (completed in white marble in 1653), but many regions of that vast country have long been noted for particular types of stonework. In Rajasthan, for example, latticework carving (or jali) made the region famous long before India became part of the British Empire.

Even in the world's most remote regions, we are never far from some kind of ancient stonework. Perhaps the most spectacular examples are the moai or carved statues of Easter Island. These massive, haunting black stone figures, carved from tuff (compressed volcanic ash), each fitted with a stone hat and bright coral eyes, stare out across the sea centuries after the last of the people who carved them disappeared. We have no certain idea why they were carved – and in such numbers.

CHANGING STYLES AND METHODS
The remains of ancient stone towers in Scotland (known as brochs) and Celtic cairns, stone circles and burial chambers often show stone used 'as found', or roughly

ABOVE *The two skins of a dry-stone wall rise up from a large foundation of stones with an even inward lean. The middle is packed with stone debris and the best stone is used for the facing. The strength of the wall comes from the large flatstones which lie about halfway up and reach through the whole width.*

it is easier to calculate load-bearing capacity and the nature of the various forces that act on a structure, as well as being easier to plan and erect the construction. European builders didn't always get it right though. The masons of many medieval churches and other buildings had to take remedial actions or alter their designs as the results of bulging or toppling walls. But such experiences merely added to the knowledge and skills of the master-builders and stonemasons of the time.

Meanwhile, stone working in Central and South America developed very different traditions from those of Europe and Asia. Many Aztec and Mayan structures, for example, show precisely-fitted blocks in their stone walls but, bizarrely, individual stones are not cut in regular blocks. Instead, each stone appears to have been carved as an individual piece in a jigsaw that allows curved stones of widely different sizes to be fitted together. It must have taken thousands of hours of slow abrasive work to make each stone fit in this way.

In Britain the stone-working techniques and tools used by the Romans fell into disuse, at least during the so-called Dark Ages when timber was often the preferred building material. It is certainly true that the seventh-, eighth- and ninth-century stone buildings that survive show less precise and regular stone use than would typically be found in a Roman building. It is as if the old skills were only just beginning to be re-learned, and even well into the eighteenth century many cottages were built of essentially undressed rough local stone, with plenty of lime mortar to fill the very variable gaps between stones of different shapes and sizes. During the Middle Ages there was a huge growth in the popularity of stone buildings across Europe; cathedrals and smaller churches as well as manor and

shaped rather than precisely cut or carved. The tradition of using rough stone continues to this day in, for example, the dry-stone walls seen as livestock-proof boundaries in many parts of Britain, from the West Country to Yorkshire. Using rough stone is a skilful business in its own right. It takes experience and a good eye to see where particular stones can best be made to fit into the overall structure in such a way that they help keep the whole edifice from collapsing. Dry-stone walls are still built without using mortar to bind the stones.

The Egyptians, Greeks and Romans developed techniques of precision stone cutting and shaping that allowed very large buildings to be created as well as colossal statues. In theory, where stone is precisely fitted in regular-shaped, right-angled blocks other substantial houses were built in large numbers. In England much of the money for this was provided by the wealth created by the wool trade. This period was perhaps the height of achievement in European stonework with continuous masons at work all over Europe on magnificent churches and cathedrals, with finely constructed and precisely fitted vaults, flying buttresses, towers and spires, covered with decorative carvings and sculptures.

The eighteenth century saw a new burst of enthusiasm for the Classical style in Britain. Tudor and Elizabethan brick gave way to a passion for finely cut stone buildings in the style advocated by the Italian Renaissance architect Antonio Palladio. Among the best surviving examples of the Palladian style in Britain is Lord Burlington's Chiswick House.

> *During the nineteenth century there was a technological revolution in masonry through the invention of Portland cement*

But by the middle decades of the nineteenth century the Gothic revival – a passion among British architects and designers for all things medieval – had largely ousted the enthusiasm for the Classical. Architects and builders insisted that Gothic was somehow a native tradition and that the Classical style, by contrast, was a foreign import. The highest expression of the Gothic revival can be found in the Palace of Westminster, completed in the 1830s to the designs of Sir Charles Barry and Augustus Welby Pugin. Pugin's passion for the Gothic bordered on the pathological, but his mania led to a profound change in taste.

Stones had been bound in place with lime mortar for centuries, – based on a mixture of lime (extracted by burning limestone) and aggregates, usually sharp sand. During the nineteenth century there was a technological revolution in masonry through the invention of Portland cement. Based on limestone but with a high content of silica and aluminium, it gradually replaced lime mortar in stone buildings. The cement was easier and quicker to use, but in renovation work lime mortar continues to have an important role.

By the end of the nineteenth century stone quarrying and cutting had certainly become easier with the introduction of power-driven saws (though much stone was

BELOW *Medieval churches and cathedrals are treasure houses of fine stonework, with carvings and sculptures as well complex architectural features, such as the fan vaulting in King's College Chapel, Cambridge, completed in about 1515.*

The stonemason uses a variety of mallets and chisels in varying sizes; the finer chisels and the smaller mallets are reserved for the most intricate and precise work. Mallets made of nylon, originally a hard wood such as fruit

still quarried by hand). Stone-carving chisels had also improved immeasurably as harder types of steel became available. But between the Classical and Gothic styles, the actual techniques of the stonemason would have remained largely unchanged – it was the designs the mason followed that had altered. Then the twentieth century passion for prefabricated steel-framed buildings led to major changes in stone-working for building. Where once solid stone had formed the walls it was now used in thin slabs as cladding or for purely decorative purposes.

STONEWORK IN BRITAIN

From ancient stone circles whose meaning still eludes us, to extraordinary stone-clad skyscrapers that rival the great pyramids and tombs of antiquity, Britain has a wealth of superb examples of the stonemason's art.

The most famous example of early stonework in Britain is without question Stonehenge. Work on the circle probably began about 3100–2900BCE, but it was unquestionably an important site for thousands of years prior to that date. Despite the difficulties of moving and erecting such huge stones in this early period, Stonehenge was completed with lintels level to within an inch, and forms an almost perfectly symmetrical circle.

Stonehenge's huge blocks of stone were shaped and secured with enormous skill: the vertical connections were created using precisely cut and shaped mortise-and-tenon joints; the horizontals used tongue-and-groove joints. How the precise stone-working was achieved using only mauls (rounded stone tools) is a mystery, as the massive stones that go to make up the circle are made from exceptionally hard stone.

The bluestones (dolerite) were probably brought from the Preseli Hills of Pembrokeshire, a distance of two hundred miles. As each stone weighed more than a ton and there were eighty in all, this was no mean feat. In a later phase of building the bluestones were removed and the much bigger sandstone sarsens we see today – each weighing more than thirty tons – were transported from the Marlborough Downs some thirty miles away.

The sarsens were arranged in an eighty-stone circle with twenty of the re-used bluestones re-erected inside the new outer circle. The outer circle was fitted with a continuous stone lintel superbly fitted to the uprights and each using those mortise-and-tenon and tongue-and-groove joints.

Far to the north of Stonehenge on the Scottish island of Mousa is another less well-known but equally remarkable example of an early stone building. One of some 500 similar stone towers, the Mousa broch was probably made between 200BCE and 200CE and still stands more than thirteen metres high, with walls nine metres thick at the base.

{ *The massive stones that go to make up the circle at Stonehenge are made from exceptionally hard stone* }

Within the massive thickness of the walls there are numerous chambers – these may

BELOW *Hadrian's Wall was a frontier built to separate the Romans and the Picts tribes in Scotland. It runs from the east to the west coast of Britain, from Wallsend in Tyneside to Bowness-on-Solway in Cumbria. The width was reduced in later parts of the build, probably to speed up the work.*

have been used for storage or for some other purpose that we can now only guess at.

Much older stone buildings are found in the Orkneys, including Neolithic settlements where the dwellings were built more than 4,000 years ago from large stone slabs. Then there is the recently discovered massive Neolithic 'cathedral', 25m (82ft) long and 20m (65ft) wide, between the Ring of Brodgar and the Stones of Stenness. The temple walls are 4.1m (16ft) thick and the furniture and artwork within are created from stone.

The Romans left Britain many stone-built treasures but few are more impressive than Hadrian's Wall, which was built from finely cut stone at the extreme northern limit of

the vast Roman Empire. The wall is nowhere higher today than about 1m (3.2ft), but when first built it would have been over 6m (20ft) high, with mile-castles, turrets and forts dotted along its eighty Roman miles (117km or 73 modern miles). Much of the stone used is hard greeny-grey dolerite.

On the south coast the Roman fort of Portchester (known to the Romans as Portus Aderni), with its splendid views out over the Solent, has the most complete Roman walls

{ *Far more Saxon stonework survives in Britain than one might imagine, mostly in churches* }

in Northern Europe, beautifully made in stone. Along the seaward front there are D-shaped bastions at intervals, designed to be fitted with Roman catapults (or ballista).

In Somerset the city of Bath manages to combine magnificent eighteenth century limestone buildings with the wonderful remains of a stone-built Roman city. Indeed Bath – or Aqua Sulis as the Romans called their new town – has one of the best preserved Roman bath complexes in Europe. At the centre of the whole complex and in its own elaborate hall was the great bath, surrounded by statues of the gods. This is the centrepiece of the baths as we see them today, though only the lower courses of the stone structure are Roman. The rest is largely Georgian.

Far more Saxon stonework survives in Britain than one might imagine, mostly in churches. In the village of Deerhurst in Gloucestershire, for example, there are two Saxon buildings. The church of St Mary with its large distinctive tower looks medieval, or perhaps Tudor, from a distance, but up close it is quickly apparent from the decorative features that this is a finely made Saxon structure. The tower has distinctive herringbone masonry details as well as curious animal head carvings. The polygonal apse is generally agreed to be ninth century work, but the earliest, rectangular part of the building was begun in the late seventh century, the apse and chapels added in the ninth century and the porch in the tenth. Just down the road is Deerhurst's other Saxon building, Odda's chapel, which is now part of a medieval farmhouse. It is tiny, with only two rooms, but still has its original window openings and its original chancel arch.

Soon after the Norman Conquest in 1066, building began on the Tower of London, but it wasn't until 1190 that work began to

encircle the famous White Tower with two walls and a moat. This work was probably complete by 1285. The White Tower itself was built from Caen stone from Northern France, specially imported at immense cost by William the Conqueror.

For many, Kenilworth Castle – the largest and some would say most impressive castle ruin in England – epitomises the image of the English medieval fortress. Building began about fifty years after the Conquest. At the heart of the castle is the inner bailey with its massive Norman keep. All the buildings that go to make up the inner parts of the castle, including the Tudor gardens, are protected

TOP *The city of Bath was built using oolitic limestone, carted out of the nearby quarries of Combe Down by horses.*
ABOVE *Odda's Chapel in Deerhurst incorporates many typical Anglo-Saxon features, including long-and-short corner stones, double-splayed windows and tall proportions.*

ABOVE *A local outcrop of good sandstone would have been a factor for selecting the location of Kenilworth Castle, which is now the largest castle ruin in England. Its Great Hall is second only in size to London's Westminster Hall.*

{ *Numerous ruined abbeys and monastic buildings are a reminder of the fine stonework produced by medieval religious houses* }

by a magnificent stone curtain wall which still has its round and polygonal towers.

A small town house completed just after the Conquest sounds too unlikely to be true, but one such house does indeed survive – and in a most unlikely setting. Halfway down one of the narrow lanes that descends from Lincoln's great cathedral is a modest looking stone house, now part of a much later row of houses and known as Jews House. Only the arcading on the front stonework of the house gives a clue to the extraordinary age of this building, for it is believed to date to the mid twelfth century – which makes it by far the oldest domestic building still in use in the country.

Numerous ruined abbeys and monastic buildings are a reminder of the fine

stonework produced by medieval religious houses. Among the finest is Fountains Abbey in Yorkshire, much of which dates to the second half of the twelfth century. Its building continued through succeeding centuries and despite the destruction of the Dissolution, much remains to remind us of the Abbey's former glory. The cellarium, where the monks' food stocks were kept, is unique – over 91m (300ft) long with beautifully ribbed stone vaulting and twenty-two bays, it is an architectural masterpiece.

Syon House, Calke Abbey, Alnwick Castle, Holkham Hall, Knole, Hardwick Hall and hundreds of equally well known early houses pay tribute to the skills of countless long-vanished stonemasons across Britain. And then there are the stone curiosities and follies, perhaps most spectacularly exemplified by Scotland's Dunmore Pineapple. Just a few miles south of Stirling, the sandstone Pineapple was completed

decorated with superb carved figures by Eric Gill (1882–1940).

Bringing the story right up to date, the Great Court at the British Museum, finished in 2000, is an example of new stone carved and fitted to match older work – although in a row that probably echoes similar disputes down the centuries the Trustees of the museum actually sourced the wrong stone for the work: they bought French limestone instead of Portland stone!

LEFT *The fine stonework of the Elizabethan Hardwick Hall in Derbyshire is maintained by a team of dedicated masons on site, using stone quarried from the estate.*

in 1761. At 14m (46ft) high it is actually a sort of gazebo – a place where the laird of Dunmore could look out across his gardens and land.

Superb, more recent, stone buildings include Lutyens' granite Castle Drogo in Devon, completed in 1930, and the dramatic Portland stone-clad Economist Building in London, completed in 1964.

In addition to its fine stone buildings Britain has a wealth of carved stone works of art. In London's Royal Academy you can see the only sculpture by Michelangelo in Britain – the Teddei Tondo or Virgin and Child with St John, carved between 1504 and 1506 from a particularly pure block of white Carrara marble. The stone sculptures of Henry Moore (1898–1986) can be seen in many settings up and down the country. The Art Deco Broadcasting House, completed in 1932 and for long the headquarters of the BBC in London, is a splendid stone building

LEFT *The building of the Dunmore Pineapple in Scotland, was planned and designed so that the leaves were cantilevered out from meticulously coursed masonry, with its last leaf some 14m (45ft) above ground level. The curving leaves were drained separately in order to prevent frost damage, and the keystone above the south entrance carries the date 1761.*

THATCHING

The Craft of Thatching

Fashioning plant material into a long-lasting and insulating roof covering for cottages and farmhouses requires the depth of knowledge and skill of the thatcher, though in times gone by most farmhands could thatch a rick to protect hay and corn. Roof thatching, in the hands of a master, gives a strong sense of place and blends with the surrounding landscape, especially in regions where its use is traditional.

For many of us, the image of the thatched cottage seems to sum up the beauty and history of the English countryside. But that is only part of the reason that, in recent years, the craft of thatching has experienced a major revival – up from an estimated two hundred thatchers in the early 1960s to roughly two thousand in 2009.

Thatching's other great appeal is that it is a craft that fits perfectly with the modern desire to reduce the damage we do to our planet. It is a craft that uses local, sustainable materials that might otherwise be wasted, to create something beautiful, useful and lasting. Thatching also strikes a deep chord in the national psyche because it harks back to a golden age of craftsmanship; an age before mass production took the pride out of creation.

Although the experience of centuries has refined the art of thatching to produce a roofing material that can hold its own against all comers, the modern thatcher's tools and equipment would still be instantly recognised by his medieval counterpart.

THATCHING MATERIALS

Thatching developed in the pre-industrial era for the simple reason that it made use of cheap local materials at a time when transport was too slow and expensive to obtain alternative materials from further away, even if the latter were better than those available locally. So thatching belongs to a splendid tradition of innovation, of making the best of whatever is to hand. Apart from turf, thatch was the only possibility for roofing until stone, slate and eventually burnt-clay tiles began to be used.

Water reed

In primitive times before arable farming, wild vegetation was used for thatching and continued to be used in more remote areas. In upland areas, for example, such as parts of Cornwall, the Lake District and the Scottish Highlands, the choice might be heather, gorse, broom or bracken, which were used to roof the cottages of the poor.

In the wetlands of East Anglia – typically the Norfolk Broads – there were plentiful

ABOVE *Many thatched houses are listed buildings and have statutory protection because they are of special historic or architectural interest.*

FAR LEFT *Water reed is found in marsh lands, waterways and tidal estuaries. The reeds can only be harvested after hard frosts have stripped the long leaves from the stems.*

LEFT *Mechanisation in agriculture saw the advent of the reaper binder and threshing machine. They produced a material from the straw with ears and butts mixed together, which has become known as long straw.*

supplies of reeds and rushes for thatching, and here water reed (*Phragmites communis*) made a marvellously desirable material for thatchers, who developed their own traditions.

Grown for centuries across the wetlands of East Anglia, water reed varies between three or four to perhaps seven or eight feet in length. The best part of the reed is the bottom, or butt end; because this grows in water it is the most durable part of the plant.

Sometimes for thatching, reed is mixed with a small proportion of bulrush to make it even more durable.

There has been combed straw thatching in the South West for at least 600 years

Sedge (*Cladium mariscus,* or great fen sedge), a plant with three-sided rush-like leaves, is also grown and harvested in East Anglia's fens and marshes: it is far more flexible than reed and is therefore used to complete the ridge on a reed-thatched roof.

Today a great deal of reed is imported, mostly from Eastern Europe, but the old hands insist that Norfolk reed is still the best.

RIGHT *Bundles of water reed should contain 99 per cent pure Phragmites – a flower head resembling a soft, feathery plume – with minimal dead leaf, and it should be bright in colour.*

Straw

With the development of crop-growing in lowland areas, straw of various kinds became a wonderful and abundant by-product of essential food production, especially wheat and rye straw, and sometimes oat straw.

Two kinds of straw thatching evolved: one using wheat 'long straw' and the other using 'combed wheat reed' which, despite its name, is not reed at all but simply wheat straw that has been 'combed' to remove debris and align the individual straw stems tidily. Combed wheat reed is often known as 'Devon reed'. There has been combed straw

LEFT *Sheaves of straw are stooked in the field and left to dry for two or three weeks after cutting. The timing of the harvest is crucial for thatching straw: if it is delayed by even a few days in hot, dry weather, the straw will ripen fully and become brittle, rendering it of little use.*

thatching in the South West for at least 600 years, and the thatching style using combed straw is distinctively neatly cropped and tight, in contrast to the more flowing style of long straw thatching found in other regions. On the finished roof, combed wheat reed looks very similar in style to Norfolk reed (hence the name) and both materials are now used in the West Country.

Longevity

It has been estimated that several hundred houses still exist in England where the underlayer of thatch – that is, the straw closest to the rafters – may have been preserved since medieval times. This is actually far more likely than at first might seem possible, because traditionally only the weathering layer – the topmost layer – of thatch is replaced when a long straw roof needs an overhaul.

There are no hard-and-fast rules about which material lasts longer on the roof, but in general the guidelines given by the Rural Development Commission back in the 1980s still hold good: water reed 50–60 years, combed wheat reed and long straw 20–30 years – but all depending on the quality of

the crop, the method of harvest, weather conditions, local environment (winds, trees and so on) and, above all, the skill of the thatcher.

HARVESTING

The harvesting of heather, gorse, bracken, various grasses and reeds for roofing in ancient times would have been carried out with simple sharp-edged manual implements or the material was just pulled by hand.

Harvesting straw

Thatching straw was originally harvested by hand as part of the cereal crop with the aid of scythes and sickles. In the nineteenth century cereal harvesting was gradually mechanised, first with horse-powered reaping machines and then with machines that could bind the sheaves at the same time as cutting the standing crop. The sheaves would eventually be taken to the farmyard to be threshed, separating the grain from the straw. Today this entire operation takes place instantly in the field with the aid of combine harvesters.

{ *Many eighteenth and nineteenth century paintings of harvest time show precisely what the old stooks looked like* }

But combines give precedence to grain and they crush the straw, so it cannot be used for thatching. The earlier machinery was less aggressive, and today straw for thatching is still harvested by reaper-binders, but tractor-powered rather than horse-drawn.

Ideally, wheat destined to produce thatching straw is harvested just before the grain is fully ripe. This ensures a higher moisture content, which reduces the risk

that the straw will become brittle. After cutting with the binder the sheaves are 'stooked' or stood up on end in the fields to dry for two or three weeks before use. Many eighteenth and nineteenth century paintings of harvest time show precisely what the old stooks looked like.

For combed wheat reed, the straw was combed by hand by gangs of women. Now it is put through a mechanised reed comber: the grain is removed without the straw going through a threshing drum, and the straw emerges clean, undamaged and with all the butts lying in one direction in a sheaf.

Harvesting Norfolk reed

Norfolk reed is cut from mid-December until early April, and the harvesting is now usually done mechanically by lawnmower-like machines or converted rice harvesters. However, 'mowing' reed by cutting it by hand is a practice that is still carried out in some areas, using a traditional hook (sickle) or a reed scythe (rather like a straight version of the long-handled scythe used for hay cutting), and cutting close to the base of the plant. The reeds are then

ABOVE *The best Norfolk reed for thatching is single wale reed, a good bundle of which will cover around a square foot on a roof. Single wale reed is cut from the beds just once a year, so the bundle will contain young, strong plants.*

LEFT *A vintage threshing machine that is still used in Oxfordshire.*

ABOVE *Despite the variations in thatching techniques, the same tools are used by thatchers. Few tools are required, and many have more than one purpose; a spar hook, for example, can be used to both split and sharpen hazel spars.*

thatcher's work really begins. As with so many crafts, much of the effort and skill goes into preparation.

Thatch of all kinds works best where the roof is steeply pitched, because a steep pitch will ensure that the water is shed quickly. In the South West, combed wheat reed roofs were traditionally less steeply pitched than, say, long straw roofs in East Anglia.

On ancient buildings the thatch might be six or more feet thick, with new layers traditionally being added on top of the old each time the roof is re-thatched, but most thatch is between 30cm and 122cm (12in and 48in) deep.

The thatcher's tools are remarkable in many ways for their sheer simplicity: a sickle-shaped shearing hook, an eaves hook or knife to trim the eaves and gable ends, a side rake for cleaning and compacting the roof, sheep shears for small trimming jobs, and a spar knife for splitting the hazel spars.

There was a time, even within living memory, when many a farm worker could turn his hand to thatching a rick, and those basic skills were developed over the centuries into the craft of the master thatcher working on buildings.

loosely bundled and 'dressed' with the aid of a simple homemade rake – essentially a piece of wood with two or three long nails protruding from it – to strip off any roots and bits of side shoots. Next, the bundle is 'knocked up' against a flat board called a leggat, to align the butt ends and make a tight bunch. The bundles are then stacked carefully on dry ground to air. Norfolk reed is still sold by the bundle, 'tied by a fathom' – a term that meant five or six bunches of reed stacked upright that could be tied with a piece of string measured at six feet long. In an average season a single reed cutter might harvest between four and six thousand bundles, making sixty to seventy bundles a day by hand. A machine can make two to three thousand bundles a day.

HOW THATCHERS WORK

Once the reed or wheat straw has been harvested and carefully stored, the

Long straw thatching

Uncombed straw (that is, traditional long straw as opposed to combed wheat reed) is prepared by shaking it out loosely on to a flat bed where it is kept damp, but not wet. A small amount of water will make the straw pliable and smooth; too much moisture and the straw will be less durable.

The bed needs to be fairly substantial and sometimes it is weighted – the weight or pressure of straw on straw helps the thatcher get a good smooth pull of straw. He will draw out double handfuls from the bottom of the pile and lay them side by side, cleaning and straightening them with all the straws pointing more or less the same way, before working the handfuls into tight compact bundles known as yealms, roughly 13–15cm (5–6in) thick and 46cm (18in) broad. These are carried up to the roof on a forked stick, or 'yoke', and pegged temporarily close to the thatcher while he is working. They are then to hand when he needs to slide them into place.

The thatcher uses sways to fix the thatch to the rafters. A sway is a hazel pole or steel rod laid horizontally across the middle of each layer of straw, which is then fixed to the roof using iron crooks, tarred cord or screw ties driven into each rafter. Where a top coat of new thatch is being added to an existing base coat (which is traditional practice), the new thatch layer is fixed to the old using spars or broaches (and there are

many other local names for these), which are split hazel or willow rods some 30 inches long and sharply pointed at each end. They are twisted into a staple shape and pressed or hammered with a wooden mallet down through both coats.

The thatcher starts at the level of the eaves and works up towards the ridge so that each layer of straw overlaps the previous layer. Long straw thatch gets its traditional and slightly shaggy appearance because the thatcher aims for a roughly 50/50 split between butts showing and heads of straw showing on the finished roof. Traditionally, long straw thatch is not shaved to tidy it up but, when a job nears completion, the thatcher will rake the straw (to remove loose

ABOVE *The more noticeable variations in thatching techniques are governed largely by the materials used, each having its own traditional methods.*

LEFT *Bent wooden spars or spics, are used for pinning one layer of thatch to another. As many as 10,000 might be used on average sized roof.*

Careful preparation is key to successful long straw thatching. The straw is laid out on a bed and dampened, ensuring that there is an even mix of heads and butts and no clumps of straw aligned the same way. The thatcher is aiming for an even split of heads and butts showing on the finished roof.

RIGHT *Long straw is distinguished by its slightly shaggy appearance. Neatly clipping the eaves and gable ends completes the job.*

BELOW *The ridge being completed using straw wrapped over the apex on a long straw thatched roof.*

bits) as well as tidily clipping the eaves and gable ends.

The Ridge

Great attention is paid to the gulleys and curves on a roof: if they are not gently rounded, water may concentrate in particular runs and cause the material to fail far more quickly than it would otherwise.

The ridge normally needs new work every eight to twelve years, because this part of the thatch has to bear the brunt of the worst of the weather. Two main types of ridge thatching techniques have developed among straw thatchers. Most widely used is the wrap-over, but in the South West the butt-up technique is used, probably to take account of the stiffer combed wheat reed. The wrap-over technique, as its name implies, involves folding a thick layer of long straw over the apex of the roof and then attaching it firmly on either side. On a butt-up ridge the thick ends of the straw are pushed together from either side to create an apex.

Many thatchers use distinct decorative diamond or other shaped thatch on the ridge of a house, but this attempt to sign one's work is a relatively modern innovation and is frowned upon for older buildings where the idea is to create, so far as possible, the look that the building would originally have had.

Apart from its soft look, long straw thatch

> *Long straw roofs are also netted to reduce the risk of damage caused by birds either nesting or looking for nesting materials*

can usually be distinguished from water reed by the exterior hazel or withy rods (liggers) used at eaves and gables. These liggers serve a practical purpose producing firm eaves and gables in the flexible material, not necessary in water reed. Long straw roofs are also netted to reduce the risk of damage caused by birds either nesting or looking for nesting

RIGHT *A leggat is beaten against the ends of the thatch stalks, driving the reed up into position. The aim is to leave only a small amount of their ends exposed so that they are parallel to the pitch of the roof. This newly thatched water reed roof uses sedge for its ridge.*

RIGHT *For Norfolk reed thatch the wooden head of a leggat is fitted with short studs, often made with horseshoe-nail heads.*

materials, a problem from which reed does not suffer.

Combed wheat (Devon) reed and water (Norfolk) reed

Combed wheat reed and Norfolk reed are fixed to the roof butt-end down, which creates a cropped look. The two materials have a similar finish, but look harsher than long straw thatch.

Combed wheat reed can be attached to an old base coat of straw, as with long straw thatching, but with water reed the whole

roof is usually stripped to the rafters and replaced when the time comes.

The basic technique of attaching reed is similar to that used by the long straw thatcher. Bundles of new reed are carried on to the roof and, starting at the lowest level, fixed to the rafters using steel or hazel sways. Once in position the reed is dressed using a legget – a square tamping device that allows the reed to be packed neatly and evenly.

When it comes to the ridge, long straw thatchers and Norfolk reed thatchers' techniques differ because water reed is too stiff and brittle to be bent over the ridge. To get round the problem the reed thatcher uses a thick layer of more flexible sedge.

OTHER USES FOR STRAW

Straw is a far more useful natural material than many might imagine. Apart from obvious uses such as bedding for animals and of course thatching, straw was the key raw material that for centuries drove much of the hat making industry.

Until the late 1950s very few men in Europe and America ventured out without a hat, and in summer the hat almost universally chosen was made from straw.

Though today it is much changed, the town of Luton grew and prospered on its hat-making businesses. Other towns, including St Albans, had similarly extensive straw hat-making industries.

{ *Straw was the key raw material that for centuries drove much of the hat making industry* }

The industry utilised the abundant straw left after the harvest in the rich arable farms that spread up through Bedfordshire and Hertfordshire into East Anglia. Some idea of the extent of the industry can be gathered

from the number of separate craft skills involved in making straw hats.

The process began when the raw straw was split along its length and plaited by hand into long strips by women and children working at home – thousands of poor cottagers added a little to their income each harvest-time in this way. The plaits might be sold on to straw plait dealers or direct to hat makers. Specialist skills in the hat making industry, which was in many ways still a cottage industry until the end of the nineteenth century, included straw-plait bleaching, straw finishing, plait milling, plait sewing, straw hat blocking and straw

ABOVE *Corn-dolly making requires the same varieties of wheat that are used by thatchers, harvested in a similar way. The straw is best used soon after cutting, but if allowed to become dry it can be damped to make it pliable and workable again.*

ABOVE *There are a number of benefits of using straw in cavity walls, in addition to the ease of construction and value for money. The straw allows the walls to breathe, as well as offering great insulation and sound proofing.*

hat stiffening. Straw plait was also stitched into mats, which have the great advantage of being cheap, warm, hard-wearing and of course biodegradable.

In Ireland, particularly in the west where timber was scarce, straw was a vital component of the chair-making business. Where rush seats tended to be used in England, straw was more common in Ireland because it was cheaper and more widely available. The sugan chair (sugan is the Irish word for straw or straw rope) was a brilliant response to the need to make the best use of whatever was locally available. In addition

to creating the seats of chairs using woven straw, the sugan maker could make a whole chair out of coiled straw rope if no wood was available.

Straw rope was made by hand on many farms in Britain by twisting straws together, with or without the help of a 'throwcock' in the barn.

Until well into the twentieth century, transport and food distribution, not to mention food production, relied almost completely on the horse, and the most important part of a working horse's harness was and is the horse-collar. This is the part against which the horse pushes, and an ill-fitting, uncomfortable collar would quickly lead to sores and a horse unable to work. The key to a good horse-collar is the straw stuffing, and even today straw is still used because nothing works quite so well.

But perhaps the best known of all straw manufacturing oddities is the corn dolly. It is said that the making of corn dollies pre-dates Christianity – the word 'dolly' is probably

> *It is said that the making of corn dollies pre-dates Christianity*

a corruption of the word 'idol', and is not connected with children's dolls (and the word 'corn' means grain, not maize). There arose variations of the corn dolly tradition right across Europe to Russia and beyond. Usually, the last sheaf of corn would be woven into a 'corn mother' and then carried back to the village or a wreath would be woven from the last corn stalks and placed on the head of the prettiest girl in the village. The corn spirit would then spend the winter in the village, before being ploughed back into the soil in the spring.

Corn dollies have a distinctive regional flavour in Britain. Styles include bells, knots, spirals, lanterns, horseshoes, fans, crowns, wreaths, crosses and chandeliers. Today the tradition continues, and straw dollies are still made up and down the country – but mostly for sale to visitors.

Less elaborate than corn dollies, small straw twists, or countryman's favours, were traditionally woven by young men in the shape of a heart and given to their

sweethearts. If the girl was next seen wearing the favour, it meant the man's love was reciprocated.

In more recent times straw has come into its own as a building material. During World War II straw-bale housing for livestock on quite a substantial scale was encouraged by the government. Sixty years later a number of houses for human habitation have been built with solid straw-bale walls. So long as the water is kept out with rendering, the straw provides superb noise and heat insulation at almost no cost beyond the labour of installing it.

ABOVE *Straw bale walls are covered with plaster on both sides and can be strong enough to hold up a snow-covered roof, and resist winds of over 100 mph (161 km).*

LEFT *The corn dolly was believed to ensure that, after harvest, the resident spirit of the crop – who had been made homeless because the wheat had all been cut down – could be persuaded to come back the following year.*

Scooping with both hands, straw is drawn from the bed, laid out out in a 'line' and then secured tightly to form a yealm – the building block or tile of a thatched roof.

MATTHEW WILLIAMS & DAVID BRAGG *have revived the traditional methods of long straw thatching in Oxfordshire.*

The Mastercrafters

Alhough it survives in parts of East Anglia, the tradition of long straw thatching had all but died out in Oxfordshire and surrounding counties until Matthew Williams and David Bragg set up Rumpelstiltskin Thatching, a company devoted to restoring the ancient tradition of long straw thatching to the region.

Matt sparkles with enthusiasm when he explains the company's mission and the thinking behind it:

'Until the canals and railways made transport cheap and easy, all thatchers used local materials and only local materials. Oxfordshire houses would have been thatched with long straw – not water reed, which only came in because transport became cheaper and because people thought stuff from farther away was better than local stuff, which, as it turned out, was largely nonsense.

'We hear about water reed thatch lasting up to eighty years. That might be true in optimum conditions with the best reed there is, but we've seen water reed that's lasted maybe eight or ten years. The problem is that huge amounts of it are imported from Poland and China, where it is often grown in polluted water. That makes for poor quality reed, which won't last. And imagine the waste of energy in transporting that inferior material half way round the world.'

Matt and Dave are eager to emphasise that long straw thatching is truly green.

> *Straw thatch is, if you like, the ultimate green material – it's a superb insulator, it uses a by-product of an important food crop and it looks great!*

'When we use wheat straw we're using something that's just a by-product of food production,' says Matt. 'We have eight acres of local wood that we coppice for our hazel spars and we're negotiating with local farmers to get them to grow the sort of wheat we need (the older varieties) so we don't have to transport it miles across country.

'Straw thatch is, if you like, the ultimate green material – it's a superb insulator, it uses a by-product of an important food crop and it looks great!'

It is not only thatch's green credentials that the men are passionate about, they are also advocates of traditional thatching techniques and honouring local styles. They are keenly aware that Oxfordshire houses look better with long straw thatch, because that is what they were built to carry. Regional styles developed because the local climate and architecture demanded that thatchers adapt their methods and materials to suit the particular conditions. So only the correct local style properly matches the buildings.

'We want to restore the traditions that existed in this part of the world before water reed and the fashion for combed reed came in from miles away. A good, well fixed long straw thatch will last maybe thirty years, which is good by comparison with all but the best water reed. But, just as important, it looks right for this area because many of

the cottages and houses we work on were designed to take long straw thatch. Even though good water reed may last as well, it demands the removal of ancient layers of thatch and therefore the loss of a part of our cultural heritage. The local long straw style lasted as long as it did – until the 1960s – simply because it worked.'

In their pursuit of authenticity Matt and Dave have learned to look deep into the past when they start work on a roof.

{ *Long straw had traditionally been the dominant thatching style throughout the Midlands and the south of England* }

'We can read an ancient roof because under the top coat of thatch on a very old house you might find straw that dates back five hundred years or more,' says Dave. 'When we get down to that level we see ancient varieties of wheat straw and occasionally rye that might have been used in a year of bad harvest. Whatever was used it had to be local because transport was slow and very expensive.'

Early on in their thatching careers both men noticed that the lower layers of thatch that had survived longest had been put on in a very different way from the method they had been taught.

'Other thatchers in the area told us that doing things the old way was just too difficult,' says Matt, 'but having seen the unbroken long straw tradition that survives in East Anglia we learned by seeing how old thatch had been put on, and slowly abandoned the combed reed techniques we'd been taught.'

Dave and Matt both studied thatching at Knuston Hall, one of the few thatching schools in the world, where long straw thatching is still taught but few trainees take up the opportunity. Here they discovered that long straw had traditionally been the dominant thatching style throughout the Midlands and the south of England. But even within long straw thatching, different counties and areas had their own distinct and decorative styles.

'It was so fascinating and it made us determined to stick to the Oxfordshire style, which was relatively straightforward and unadorned – but it is the right style for our area.'

Much that has to do with thatching is counter intuitive, says Dave. For example, hot dry weather is actually bad for thatch.

'It lasts much longer if it's constantly wet!' he says with a smile. 'When it's wet it doesn't get brittle, which is what happens when it is too hot and dry. That's why the south-facing,

ABOVE *One of the 7,000 spars being used to attach long straw to this roof.*

BELOW *The shaggy eaves and gables are cut to a sharp finish with a traditional knife.*

sunny side of a roof always wears faster than the north side.'

The process of thatching a roof is as traditional as the materials used. With water reed thatching, the whole roof is stripped when the roof needs to be replaced. With long straw, the historically fascinating layers are left in place, as Matt explains:

'We take the old roof down until it's perhaps 45cm or 60cm (18in or 24in) thick. We then consolidate what's left till it's the right shape for us. We firm it up and fill in the dips. We then take what we call the boltings – bundles of trussed straw; we open them and lay them out on a bed. As the straw is laid down it is wetted but not too much. The water makes the straw pliable; it makes it relax, if you like. Leaving it wet also helps the sugars in the straw to ferment, we believe, so that when it's on the roof it doesn't allow damaging fungi to grow – fungi love sugar. With the sugars gone the straw becomes acid, which the bugs don't like. Once on the roof the straw actually gets stronger as it ages – it becomes ropey and tough.

'After the straw has been placed in the bed it's pulled out and gathered into yealms or handfuls and these are carried up on to the roof. Starting at the eaves, each course of straw is pegged into the roof overlaying the previous course, working gradually up to the ridge. We do the whole of one side of the roof then the other, then the heads – the straw left sticking up above the ridge is pushed over from either side to create a waterproof finish.'

Despite more farmers moving to organic production, long straw varieties are still rare due to unhelpful legislation on the varieties

ABOVE *'Oversailing' straw is wrapped over the apex and secured with spars in preparation for ridging.*

that are legally permitted to be grown. Growing their own may ultimately be the solution; Matt and Dave already produce their own hazel for the spars.

'We also have our own reaper-binder and threshing machine – they're more than half a century old but still work,' says Dave with a smile. 'We can't use straw that's been through a combine, because it destroys the straw, but the reaper-binder is perfect: it cuts the wheat and bundles it perfectly for us to leave in stooks in the field. We have to cut early so the crop is still green, because that leaves the straw still strong and pliable.'

Another problem for master thatchers like Matt and Dave is that absolutely anyone can set up a thatching business: there are no regulations that say you have to have a specific qualification. This makes it difficult for the potential customer to judge which thatcher really knows his stuff, and Dave and Matt regularly see poor quality work.

Starting Rumpelstiltskin Thatching was no easy task as there were no examples of long straw thatching for potential customers to see.

'People were understandably suspicious of us wanting to use this traditional method when they didn't know what the roof would look like or how long it would last.'

They were so confident in their methods though that they thatched their first few long straw roofs at prices that their clients couldn't turn down, knowing that they would be delighted by the results and word would quickly spread.

Matt and Dave have a simple explanation for the company's unusual name:

'If you remember the children's story, you'll know that Rumpelstiltskin was the only person who could spin gold from straw. That's what we like to think we're doing!'

> *People were suspicious of us wanting to use this traditional method when they didn't know what the roof would look like or how long it would last*

Steel 'side pins' or 'needles' are used to create a temporary brace against which the yealms can be packed. They are then secured to the older layers of thatch beneath with hazel

The Tradition of Thatching

All over the world, in temperate and tropical climates, local plant materials
have been used since earliest times to thatch roofs and make the walls of
dwellings – think of circular African tribal huts, or Pacific island homes. The
tradition has travelled full circle: there is now a thriving industry supplying
bespoke 'African' and 'Bali' hut-type structures for European, Australian and
American gardens using exotic grasses such as alang alang and Cape reed.

Thatching of one kind or another is extremely ancient, and was probably the earliest type of roofing in several parts of the world. For example, the conical roofs of traditional African huts were thatched with grasses, and in tropical countries of the Far East palm fronds were woven for roofing.

Archaeological evidence from the Iron Age circular huts at Ty Mawr near Holyhead in North Wales strongly indicates thatched roofs of some kind, and this site seems to have been more or less continually occupied from the Middle Stone Age until the sixth century CE. Early thatch in different parts of Britain will certainly have included grass, reeds, wheat straw, rushes, broom and heather and sites such as Wicken Fen in Cambridgeshire have revealed evidence of similar roofing materials – archaeologists believe one thatched hut here dates to 370 BCE.

Heather, straw and grass thatched cottages were still widespread in Ireland before the Great Famine (1845–1849), and in Scotland before the Highland Clearances of the nineteenth century. In parts of Ireland until well within living memory, the thatch on those cottages that remained was held down using long home-made straw ropes with weights attached at either end. These would be thrown over the thatch – both over the ridge and in parallel to it. The weights hanging down the walls would ensure that the ropes, and therefore also the thatch, stayed in place. Loose straw was spread over the thatch before the ropes were added, to prevent them cutting into the thatch proper. This style was mostly used in the windswept west of Ireland, but it was common too in parts of Scotland. Most Irish thatch at this time was laid on top of a layer of sods of earth. This peasant style of thatching no doubt had its counterparts in many parts of Europe during earlier periods.

Archaeobotanists, who study the past using plant remains, have examined a number of venerable thatched buildings in Devon and Northamptonshire. Their underlayers of straw, blackened by smoke from domestic hearths in the days before there were chimneys, have revealed seeds and plant varieties that strongly indicate the thatch has survived in situ since the fifteenth and sixteenth centuries.

ABOVE *Thatch was the most common roofing material during the medieval period in Britain. It remained popular until the late nineteenth century when mass production and the expansion of the railway network gradually reduced the price of other materials, such as clay tiles.*

LEFT *There are distinct regional styles of thatching, and variations occur particularly when one style has been adopted by local thatchers and handed down through generations.*

FAR LEFT *Over the past five hundred years a wide variety of materials has been used to form weathering coats of thatch, depending on traditions and availability.*

LEARNING FROM EXPERIENCE

Thatching techniques have evolved gradually and regionally, rather than in dramatic leaps. Perhaps the most striking change has been in the past few decades.

The biggest difficulty for thatchers working in a world dominated by modern chemical farming is obtaining a good supply of suitable straw. Straw for thatching needs to be of good length, which is a problem in modern arable farming where the trend has been to see straw as a waste product that needs to be minimised. For the modern thatcher, today's wheat varieties are simply not up to the job, because they were developed (mostly during the second half of the twentieth century) to produce high yields of grain, regardless of the quality or length of their stems. Varieties of wheat now have much shorter and pithier stems to prevent the crop from 'lodging' before harvest, instead of being long and hollow as straw stems used to be. Modern dwarf wheat varieties just do not grow tall enough to produce the roughly 122cm-long (48in) straw that makes ideal roofing material. Older varieties of wheat, including Square Headed Master and Little Josh, are ideal simply because they still have these long, strong stems.

But even these old varieties will fail the thatching test if they are grown using nitrogen-rich fertilisers. Modern farming practices seek to boost grain yields with liberal applications of nitrogen fertiliser, which encourages faster and therefore weaker growth of the straw. Too much fertiliser will reduce the thickness of the stem walls, making the straw unsuitable as a roofing material.

There is a substantial shortage of slowly grown, strong, long thatching straw, and thatchers try to encourage local farmers to specialise in producing straw specifically for thatched roofs. That means growing the old varieties, avoiding excessive use of artificial fertilisers, and using special and kinder machinery for harvesting and threshing the straw. Farmers, thatchers and conservation bodies are working together for the future of thatching.

> *The biggest difficulty for thatchers working in a world dominated by modern chemical farming is obtaining a good supply of suitable straw*

RIGHT *Before the 1500s thatched roofs were moderately simple in design. Changes to the design of houses after this time – with chimney stacks protruding through the roof and the upper floors better lit – made the work of the thatcher more complicated.*

CENTURIES OF THATCH

There are many fine examples of thatched houses and cottages in Britain, but they tend to be concentrated in East Anglia, in parts of the Midlands and in the South West.

Historically, thatch tended to be the roofing material used by poorer people, so there are few examples of very large houses, let alone stately homes, with thatched roofs. One of the most significant aspects of building in Britain was that the lord of the manor showed his wealth and status by deliberately using building materials that other local people could not afford. So when timber and thatch were the predominant building materials for houses, the local landowner would often choose highly expensive brick for his house, or stone, and with a roof to match.

However, a curious byway of thatching's history is that during the Picturesque Movement of the eighteenth century a fashion arose for building small houses designed to hint at a rustic idyll to which real working-class rural life bore little relation – the so-called cottage orné. Thatch was vital to the look, which is why odd thatched cottages in the grounds of big estates can still be seen in areas of the country where thatch was never the traditional roofing material. Sometimes a quite substantial mansion would masquerade as a cottage orné, but was subsequently engulfed in an even grander building, such as Hollycombe House in West Sussex: the original 'rustic' thatched house, finished in 1802 and with 'Elizabethan' chimneys, had eight bedrooms, a 6.4m (21ft) billiard room, 7m (23ft) library and 8.5m (28ft) dining room, several other very large reception rooms, a 'noble' inner hall, ample servants' quarters, aviary,

BELOW *Combed wheat reed and water reed thatch need a 'kick', or upwards tilt, at the eaves and verges. Traditionally there have been numerous different ways of achieving this, such as tightening the rods.*

conservatory and more (all thatched), but the whole edifice was subsequently enveloped by a castellated stone mansion in the 1890s. An excellent early example of the cottage orné is Queen Charlotte's Cottage at Kew in West London. The cottage, probably completed in the mid-1700s, was designed as a kind of adult playhouse where Charlotte kept exotic animals, including the first kangaroos in Britain.

The best examples of modern thatch tend to occur where groups of houses and cottages present a picture of architectural consistency; a picture that reflects the continuity of a style of roofing that is quintessentially English. True, the thatch that we are looking at will not be more than half a century old in the main, but underneath that top coat that looks so solid there may well be traces of thatch that were put on before the Reformation, and it may lie on timbers that are even older.

Perhaps the best place to start any tour of the best of British thatch is in Devon where in a village such as Dunsford the grouping of the houses shows an ancient pattern of growth that is essentially organic, and reveals what much of England would have looked like when all local communities used local building materials.

> *The best examples of modern thatch tend to occur where groups of houses and cottages present a picture of architectural consistency*

After securing a firm foundation of straw at the eaves, the thatcher then proceeds layer by layer up the roof to the apex before starting again on the other side. Straw bent over to form the ridge then provides the final weather proofing, and the eaves and gables can be neatly trimmed

ABOVE *The 36 quaint, white-washed, thatched cottages in Milton Abbas feature on many postcards of rural Dorset.*

ABOVE *Thatch on new buildings extends the local tradition into the twenty-first century and provides energy-efficient roofing that fits into the local landscape, such as this house in Walberswick, Suffolk.*

Finchingfield in Essex has a similar pattern of village growth distributed fairly evenly round a splendid green, and there are enough thatched houses to show how this part of Essex might once have looked.

All Saints Church at Salhouse in Norfolk is a good example of a now rare phenomenon – the thatched church. At Avebury in Wiltshire the seventeenth century threshing barn has a superb thatched roof and shows how the giant tithe barns of many communities

would once have looked. Also at Avebury is a delightful curiosity – a stretch of ancient thatched wall! Here the thatch nicely keeps the rain out of the mortar.

At Sturminster Marshall in Dorset there is an interesting row of small workers' cottages opposite the church. These hug the curving road and represent a short thatched terrace. In the same county another fascinating thatched village that has changed little in two hundred years and shows a unique arrangement of houses is Milton Abbas. Here the original village (strictly speaking Milton Abbas is actually a town) was completely demolished and rebuilt in the eighteenth century when the abbey from which the village gets its name decided that the smelly, noisy townspeople were simply too close for the monks to enjoy their contemplative life undisturbed. They razed the original village to the ground and moved it further up the chalky hill, where it remains to this day. Milton Abbas is an example, if you like, of an early planned town. The identical thatched houses line each side of the gently sloping street and behind them rises the spectacular high chalk escarpment.

Apart from planned villages such as Milton Abbas and the ancient villages of Devon and East Anglia, there are splendid but more isolated examples of thatched houses dotted about the country from Northampton to Hereford, Kent to Cornwall. One particularly delightful 'thatched walk' would take you along the Winterbourne stream in Dorset. Here fine examples of thatch may be seen in all the Winterbourne villages – Abbas, Steepleton, St Martin, Monckton – strung out along the stream.

What is marvellous about thatch is that every now and then someone will decide that the aesthetic qualities of straw or reed combined with its superb insulating properties is good enough reason to thatch a house in a village where perhaps no thatch has been seen in a century and more. In the seaside village of Walberswick, in Suffolk, for example, there is just one beautifully thatched house – but who knows, wherever one appears others may follow, for thatching is an ancient art that refuses to die.

> *Currently there are about 24,000 listed thatched buildings in England*

LEFT *Thatch's green credentials make it an ideal modern building material and not necessarily just for historic or nostalgic buildings. The beach houses of South Africa's Hermanus Bay were the inspiration for the thatched roundhouses at Interton-on-Sea, Norfolk.*

WOODWORK

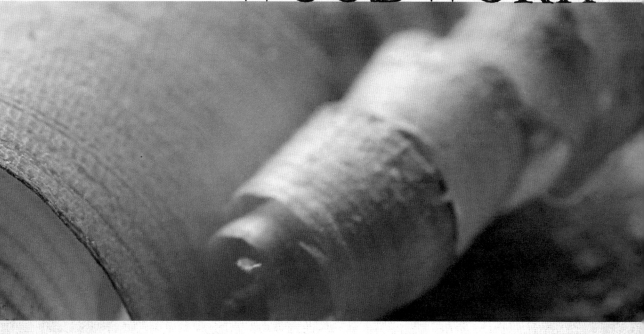

The Craft of Woodwork

Wood is one of the world's greatest and most versatile materials; indeed without it, human life would be unimaginably different. It has always been essential in everyday life providing the basic material for building shelter and making useful items of every description.

Wood is a renewable resource: you can always grow more of it. Britain was well supplied with native timber trees like oak, elm and ash but such was the demand for wood in Britain that even by the early medieval period the country's main source of hardwood timber – the vast broadleaf forests of lowland England – had been substantially reduced. The trees were felled to clear land for agriculture and to harvest for building work, fuel for local industries and home heating, and the multitude of other uses to which wood was put. Nevertheless, enough oak remained to build the English naval fleets that defeated the invading Spanish Armada in 1588, and to build so many of the magnificent church roofs and the timber-framed houses and cottages we still see across East Anglia, parts of the west Midlands, the Weald and other regions where stone was not the local building material, or where brick was not yet available in affordable quantities.

By the eighteenth and nineteenth centuries softwood (conifer) timber – particularly pine, known as deal from the Dutch deel meaning plank – was being imported on a large scale from Scandinavia and the Baltic, which had been sources of pine for Britain since the Middle Ages. Houses that would once have had oak floorboards, windows and furniture now often had pine simply because it was cheaper. Exotic woods, such as mahogany and teak, or rare woods such as ebony for inlay and other fine specialist work, were being imported from Britain's colonies; it is claimed that Sir Walter Raleigh was the first to introduce mahogany in about 1597, when he used it in the Caribbean to repair his ship.

As well as timber from large trees, a vital and sustainable source of wood for a wide range of craftsmen came from the underwood species like hazel, birch and willow. 'Underwood' generally refers to small trees, but can also include the big timber species in systems where they are cut when much younger and smaller than full-size timber trees – especially ash, oak and sweet chestnut. The system is known as coppicing, in which the young maiden tree is cut down to the stump and the stump is then allowed to regenerate, producing multiple new 'poles' after each cut. The poles are harvested on a regular cycle (varying from just a couple of years for walking sticks and basketry to perhaps 10–15 years for larger poles), and the same stump continues to produce poles for a century or more.

WOOD FROM THE TREES

Traditionally, in Britain, trees and coppice stems are felled in winter. In spring and summer the timber would be full of sap,

LEFT *Oak, a dominant native tree, is found throughout the British Isles. It is a relatively slow growing tree, reaching an average of 40m (131ft) in height.*

ABOVE *Without coppicing the hazel's life span would be between 50–70 years. The lack of a single stem or trunk means that it is generally classified as a bush rather than a tree.*

whose sugar and starch would be the perfect diet for destructive fungi in felled wood, and it would need to be dried for far longer after being cut.

The most ancient implements for felling were axes – at first stone-headed but later of iron and steel, and the latter were still used in tree felling in the early years of the twentieth century. Once an opening 'birdsmouth' had been chopped out of the tree with an axe, a two-man cross-cut saw was pulled manually back and forth to complete the felling. Chainsaws were not commonly seen in Britain's woodland until the 1960s.

The skill in felling was to cut as low as possible to ensure maximum timber recovery. Wedges might be used to ensure that the tree fell in a predictable way. The straightness and general suitability of each tree for building or furniture making would have been assessed before it was cut down. Many trees that look perfectly usable to the untrained eye would be rejected by the experienced woodsman – signs of disease or a lack of straightness might be serious problems, for example.

With the side branches removed, the main trunk was reduced to beams and planks.

> { *The skill in felling was to cut as low as possible to ensure maximum timber recovery* }

Originally this would have been another job for axes that cleaved and hewed the trunk. For building timber, whole trunks of mature trees might be simply squared off to create the massive beams so typical of early timber-framed houses.

Long before mechanisation, planks were created by a slow process that involved a sawpit – in essence a hole in the ground about 1.8m (6ft) deep. The tree would be positioned above the sawpit on cross-beams and held in place using special irons. One man would stand on the tree trunk while another stood in the pit immediately below him. The two men pulled the blade of the long vertical pitsaw up and down between them, gradually slicing the log into planks of the required length and thickness. It was incredibly slow compared with machine cutting, but skilled cutters could produce planks that were even throughout their length. They could also cut planks thin enough for veneer, using large framed saws with very thin blades.

Traditionally, the timber produced at a sawpit would be stacked with blocks between each plank to allow the air to

circulate naturally for a seasoning period that might last several years. Today the timber is sawn mechanically at the mill and some of it will be kiln-dried to speed up the seasoning process. Softwoods such as pine and spruce are now felled and stripped of their branches by huge machines.

But whatever its origin the method of converting the tree into manageable pieces, wood of every kind in the hands of a master would be transformed into something of lasting usefulness, value or beauty.

WORKING WITH WOOD

As you would expect, serving the basic human desire for shelter, building is one of the oldest applications for woodcraft. The traditional trade breaks down into carpenters who worked with large structural items such as beams and timber frames, and joiners who were responsible for the smaller components such as doors, staircases and window frames. Massive timbers would be used for sill beams, uprights, roof timbers and trusses.

For house building simple traditions developed that involved the shaping and utilising of major structural timbers, but the skill of this traditional carpentry can be seen at its best in the supporting structures of some of Britain's magnificent cathedrals, churches and vast monastic barns with complex wooden structures bridging enormous spans. Doors and window frames were more rudimentary until sash windows and panelled doors extended the skills of the joiner in recent centuries.

The tools of the medieval woodworker were remarkably like modern ones – gouges with curved rims, a range of chisels and planes and assorted mallets (wooden mallets for tapping wooden-handled tools and pegs, iron-headed hammers for nails).

Early illustrations show carpenters working with tools similar to those they would use today, but the medieval

ABOVE *There are many varieties of willow, but the most suitable for making cricket bats is* **Salix alba caerulea.** *The clefts of willow are stacked for seasoning, so that the willow loses more than half its weight in moisture, which can take up to 12 months.*

ABOVE *Angel roofs are an example of late medieval architecture. The ends of the beams were carved as angels, as seen on this hammer-beam roof at the church of Our Lady St Mary, Norfolk.*

RIGHT *The drawknife has a large range of uses, from stripping rough timber to putting decorative chamfers on furniture.*

side-axe, broadly similar to other axes but with the bevelled cutting edge on one side of the blade only, and the handle slightly offset to avoid grazing the knuckles. Hewing marks, whether by adze or more usually by side-axe, can still be seen on thousands of roof and ceiling beams in houses up and down Britain.

Other axes came in assorted sizes and blade shapes for different crafts and purposes. In the underwood crafts, side-axes, froes, billhooks, draw-knives (or

> *Boiled animal hides, hooves and tendons yielded a glue that would move with the wood*

draw-shaves) and spokeshaves were much in evidence, as well as wedges, beetles and cleaving irons. They also used shavehorses – homemade wooden benches on which the craftsman sat astride and operated a foot control that clamped the piece of wood while he shaved it clean.

The auger is no longer seen, but this primitive drill was used to make all-important peg holes, whether the object under construction was a magnificent church roof or a humble domestic chest.

The medieval bow saw was adjustable: it had an H-shaped ash frame and the tension on the string running across the top of the H, opposite the blade, could be tightened by a torsion peg whenever necessary. This meant that a thinner and more precise blade could be used because it would be held stiff by the tension of the string. Bow saws are still in use today, though not necessarily string-tensioned. Craftsmen had a variety of other small saws for intricate work – frame saws, fretsaws, jigsaws, turning saws, dowel saws, felloe saws and more.

woodworker also used the broad-axe for roughly shaping timber, and the adze for quickly smoothing the surface of larger pieces.

An adze is rather like an axe but with a dished blade, fixed at right angles to the haft rather than in line with it. In skilled hands this tool would quickly produce a reasonably smooth surface. It was typically used to hollow out the shaped seat of a Windsor chair, and different woodworking crafts had their own versions and sizes of adze. To use an adze, the craftsman stood astride his work and wielded the tool from front to back between his legs (one foot back, the other forward) – hence the curve of the blade to take account of the swinging movement. A more common carpenter's tool was the

WOOD FOR EVERY USE

Inside the buildings, furniture evolved from simple stools, benches and roughly fashioned boxes to the very fine joinery seen in later chairs, tables and cabinets (cupboards, chests, bookcases and the like).

Modern factory furniture-makers use powerful chemical glues, whereas older makers used boiled animal hides, hooves and tendons. This yielded a glue that would move with the wood as it expanded and contracted in winter and summer, so as well as keeping the joints in good order it would hold veneers down and prevent them splitting. The glue was used hot and allowed a joint to be taken apart again if that became necessary. This wood glue was gentler than modern glues, but there was an unexpected problem: it lost its grip at high temperatures or where there was high humidity, which is why eighteenth century furniture that was shipped to India and other hotter climates tended to warp and eventually fall apart.

As furniture-makers, skills became more intricate, veneers began to be used – thinly sliced layers of expensive woods that are used to cover and decorate cheaper woods. Considerable skills are involved for veneer, both in slicing the sections from the tree trunk and in applying them to the cabinet. Traditionally, veneers were cut from suitably grained wood: the better or more complex the grain, the more the furniture maker would pay. A wide variety of native and imported woods are used for veneers.

With perfectly smooth and fine-grained surfaces, cabinet makers could also create highly polished finishes, the art of wood polishing reaching its peak in the Victorian obsession with French polishing – a technique for building up layers of hard wax polish into a mirror-like sheen.

Combining small pieces of veneer to form patterns and pictures on furniture and boxes

ABOVE *Marquetry techniques involve drawing the design on paper and transferring it to the wood by needle-pricking the outlines.*

RIGHT *Grinling Gibbons introduced a curvilinear rhythm in his work that had not been seen in England. Graceful garlands of flowers, such as those at Petworth House in Sussex, became part of Gibbons' trademark.*

is known as marquetry and requires very special practical skills, along with an artistic eye to combine the different colours and grains of the woods. Parquetry is a term for formal geometric patterns, which can be created using either veneers on furniture or blocks of wood arranged in regular patterns (such as herringbone) for flooring.

The principles of veneering informs modern furniture-making at its worst, using pieces of chipboard (compressed sawdust or woodchips bonded with resin) screwed and glued together, then covered with ultra-thin fake veneers or laminate surfaces.

Turning and carving

English religious art and iconography provided the impetus for a huge craft industry of statue carving, using mostly oak and some limewood, from the end of the so-called Dark Ages until the Reformation in the sixteenth century.

Smaller wooden carvings for the home and private devotion were carved from extremely hard boxwood. The skills of these carvers,

{ *Turners value the grain and natural patterns in the wood* }

using simple gouges and chisels, were very different from the skills of the house builder or furniture maker.

Wood carving reached its apogée in the work of Grinling Gibbons (1648–1721), who created dazzling trompe l'oeil effects using mostly limewood, which he chose because it is largely free of knots, as well as being soft and easy to carve. Examples of his work exist in a number of English country houses and at Hampton Court Palace. He carved everything from lace cravats to bunches of flowers, with a skill that has never been equalled. In his workshop there was an astonishing number of chisels, with blade widths varying from less than an eighth of an inch to an inch or more across. A similar range of gouges would also have also been used. Legend has it that he always carved a pea pod somewhere in each commission and if the pod had not been carved open to reveal the peas inside it meant he had not been paid properly for the work!

The satisfying and versatile craft of 'turning' involves rotating a 'billet' of wood on a lathe and applying chisel blades as it turns, to remove the wood into something rounded such as a chair leg, a bowl or a wheel hub. The range of domestic items in turnery is considerable, and often intricate in the patterns that can be gouged into the wood as it spins.

Turners value the grain and natural patterns in the woods they use, and these are many and varied. They might even delight in diseased or damaged wood: burl or burr, for example, is fashioned from the large swirling wart-like growths sometimes seen on trees, particularly walnut and oak.

Resonant wood

Musical instrument-making is perhaps the most complex and specialist of all the types of woodcraft. The making of both stringed and wind instruments calls for incredible skill

The wood for chairmaking is cleft by driving a 'froe' into it and levering it apart so that it splits along the grain. It can then be trimmed roughly with a side axe and more finely-tuned on the shave horse with a drawknife.

instrument rather than the beauty of its construction, and it is perhaps for this reason that this is one of the few branches of woodcraft in which mechanisation has made few inroads, at least at the top end of the market. High quality guitar-making is in particular demand today, with a number of craftsmen around the world making superb quality instruments for which, despite very high prices, they have waiting lists of several years.

GREEN WOOD AND UNDERWOOD CRAFTS

Turning is one of the key processes of traditional country chair making which, despite its obvious links with general furniture, has always been a distinct branch of woodwork. Chair making was centred in several areas in Britain, but especially High Wycombe in Buckinghamshire, where the beech woods high on the Chilterns supplied the main timber for an industry based largely on individual 'bodgers', as the men in the woods who used simple homemade lathes to turn chair legs and spindles were known. The bodgers supplied the town's chair-making workshops and factories, where seats, back slats and other components would be shaped by different craftsmen from 'green' wood – that is to say wood that has not been seasoned or dried out first, but retains its sap and is thus much softer and easier to work. The later movement of the wood as it dries must be taken into account and is actually used to great advantage, the drying of the wood actually tightening the joints so no glue is required, and giving the chair great flexibility and strength.

Among the simplest and certainly one of the oldest ways to work wood is by turning it using a pole lathe, a device still used by a few craftsmen in Britain and typically by the traditional bodger to make chair legs.

ABOVE *A violin consists of about 70 different parts made of several kinds of wood. Each piece is hand-carved and made without any mechanical aids.*

RIGHT *A classic woodman's tool is the pole lathe. The treadle is connected by a cord, wrapped around the work, so that a sapling bends above the head of the operator.*

and precision. Violin makers, for example, use spruce, maple, willow and decorative dense hardwoods like ebony, rosewood and boxwood, and work with minute accuracy to produce the sculpted curve of the top and bottom of the instrument for optimum resonance, as well as the fine carving and inlay work known as purfling.

The great musical instrument-makers such as Guarneri and Stradivari treated their wood with borax and a varnish made from honey, egg white and gum, a treatment that many believe contributes to their unique sound.

Instument-making reveals another great quality of wood: its resonance; colouring and amplifying sound. The great instrument maker is judged by the sound of their

It is difficult to describe exactly how a pole lathe works, though to see one in action is to realise it is simplicity itself. A springy sapling is found and a cord is attached to its tip. The cord is then wrapped around the billet of wood on the lathe and finally attached to a treadle. When the lathe operator depresses the treadle with his foot, the top of the sapling is drawn down under tension and the cord rotates the billet. When the pedal is released, the tension is released and the sapling springs back to the straight position with some force while the cord rotates the lathe in the other direction by pulling upwards. The faster the pedalling, the faster the wood rotates. Meanwhile the craftsman's various chisels are cutting and shaping the revolving billet of wood.

All lathes work in a similar way, whether driven by water power, steam, hand or by electricity. The block of wood to be turned

{ *Guarneri and Stradivari treated their wood with borax and a varnish made from honey, egg white and gum* }

is bolted to the lathe, which then turns rapidly while a chosen chisel – braced on a special section of the lathe – is eased very slowly toward the turning surface of the wood, gradually removing layer after layer. The ultimate skills of the wood turner can perhaps best be seen in the fantastically elaborate bobbin chairs produced in the sixteenth and seventeenth centuries.

The huge range of traditional underwood crafts, often carried out under homemade shelters in the woods or in cottage workshops, had their own well-defined set of skills and disciplines, and supplied useful items such as besom brooms (using bundled birch twigs or heather), wooden hay rakes,

walking sticks, scythe handles, chair parts, barrel hoops and charcoal.

The techniques included skilled use of a wide range of edge tools to cut and shape the wood, and unusual processes such as steaming the wood so that it could be curved to form hooked walking sticks, snaking scythe handles, chair-back arches and so on.

The woven-wood crafts occupied another niche. Light woven fence panels or hurdles, fashioned from coppiced willow, hazel or other locally available species, were in huge demand to keep stock (especially sheep)

> *Split wood is stronger because it follows the grain of the timber rather than slicing across the fibres*

enclosed, but eventually gave way to wire sheep netting. Willow, being flexible, fast growing and in large supply, was also used by skilled craftsmen in the Fens and the Somerset Levels to weave baskets of every shape and size, as well as salmon putchers and eel hives (conical-shaped traps).

Clog-making combined underwood and workshop skills. Until the end of the steam era in Britain many railwaymen – particularly those working in the shunting sheds – wore wooden clogs to protect their feet from heavy objects. Factory workers customarily wore clogs and so did agricultural workers to lift their feet out of the mud or clear of wet dairy floors. Clogs were traditionally made in the north of England and carved from solid blocks of wood, usually alder (which lasted well in wet conditions underfoot) or sycamore, shaped to follow the undulations of the arched foot so that the soles allowed

LEFT *An hour or more in a steam chamber, depending on thickness, makes wood pliable enough to bend over a former and clamp into a new shape.*

the foot to rock during walking. The clog industry was a specialised one, and divided between itinerant cloggers in the woods and clog-makers in the workshops. Cloggers felled the trees, cut the trunks into short lengths, split the logs and roughly shaped the pieces into clog soles. Clog-makers, on the other hand, fine-tuned the wooden soles and made up and fitted the leather uppers and iron sole rims.

Wood-weaving and baskets

In the 1920s and 1930s, hundreds or perhaps thousands of men were making Somerset willow hurdles to meet the nationwide demand from farmers. The willow was harvested any time between October and the end of March, and trimmed into pieces 0.9–1.5m (3–5ft) long. These rods were boiled for two hours to make them pliable, and then intertwined by hand around uprights. Hurdles made in hazel in other parts of the country required horny hands, strong wrists and a lifetime of experience to weave the long hazel rods (either in the round or split by hand) tidily around the uprights, and then at the end of the row to twist them back on themselves to continue the next row.

Making a swill basket was a complicated business, but it was based on oak that had been split or riven rather than sawn. Split wood is stronger because it follows the grain of the timber rather than slicing across the fibres. A steamed hazel rod was bent and fixed into an oval shape, and split oak laths were then woven below the rod to create an incredibly strong basket that was traditionally used for carrying coal or potatoes.

There has been something of a revival in Sussex trug making which, like swill basket making, involves splitting rather than cutting the main parts. The trug boards – the flat slats from which the body of the trug is made – are of willow, soaked to make the material pliable enough to be shaped and then nailed to the frame. The hoops (frames) and handles are formed from sweet chestnut coppiced in local woodland and cleaved with a froe or cleaving axe, then smoothed down with a drawknife and steamed so that they can be bent into shape.

CARRIAGE BY WOOD

Timber was the only reliable material from which boats could be made before the introduction of modern marine plywood, steel and fibreglass, and a highly-skilled craft developed from the simplest wooden rafts, fishing boats and hyde-covered coracles to the highly sophisticated wooden sailing ships of the eighteenth and nineteenth century. In England oak was central to shipbuilding for centuries, but by the nineteenth century cedar was also being used along with mahogany,

ABOVE *Beech is a popular material for clogs as it is plentiful and well suited to machine processing.*
BELOW *The frame and handle of a trug are set in jigs and tacked together with split-oak slat.*

teak for decking and a range of other exotic woods, including iroko.

Boatbuilding has always been a distinct area of woodcraft. Here the skill lies in selecting and preparing timber to create that most traditional of boats, the clinker-built craft, where overlapping pieces of timber are caulked (made waterproof) using tar and oakum or cotton driven into the slight gaps between the overlapping planks to make them waterproof. Today marine ply is used for much boatbuilding, and the old solid wood skills are vanishing.

Wheelwrighting and coach-making

For centuries the wainwright, coach-maker and wheelwright kept the pre-industrial world moving, whether in two-wheeled farm carts, heavy four-wheeled wagons, mail and staging coaches or fine London carriages. Often the same workshop made both the body of the vehicle and its wheels and their working methods are particularly fascinating. Take the simple cartwheel, for example. A wooden wheel, however well put together, would quickly be jolted apart when a heavy load moved along a rough cobbled street or rutted country lane. To avoid this the wheelwright, often working together with a neighbouring blacksmith, would make a metal band for the outside edge of his cartwheel. This tyre would be made slightly too small for the wooden wheel rim. To make the final fit the wheelwright would heat the metal until it was red-hot (which would make it expand) and then hammer it on to the wooden rim. The whole thing would then be dipped in cold water in a hissing cloud of steam:

> *To make the final fit the wheelwright would heat the metal until it was red-hot and then hammer it on to the wooden rim*

ABOVE *Oak is a popular material to construct timber sleepers. This can be problematic due to its tendency to rot, particularly near the points where the ties are fastened to the rails.*
RIGHT *'Treen' refers to small handmade functional household objects made of wood, such as this antique wooden shaker.*

The coach-maker's ability to shape and join wood remained much in demand in the early twentieth century, adapting to new demands. Timber had always been used to make the basic framework for railway carriages when they developed out of the old mail coach, but now it was also needed for cars, buses, lorries and the new flying machines that were made with a light but strong timber framework.

A WORLD OF WOOD

Before the advent of plastic and cheap steel, the woodcrafter was at work in every sphere of human life. Homes were filled with a huge range of useful and decorative objects (known as 'treen') often made from locally available beech, sycamore and box wood. Everyday items like plates, pots, bowls, cups, shoehorns, egg cups, rolling pins, spoons, furniture knobs, chopping boards, penholders, brush backs and candlesticks; all were made from wood. Smaller decorative items – particularly snuff boxes – could be beautifully made, often in a variety of hard and soft woods. For smokers the old-fashioned clay pipe gave way to wooden tobacco pipes made in a variety of rare and unusual timbers, including the white heath tree (or Mediterranean tree heath, *Erica arborea*). Using extremely hard species such as lignum, even clock movements were sometimes made in wood. In the houses of the wealthy, the walls of the rooms were lined with oak panelling or wainscot, as it was known, and many churches had wooden wall panelling to hide the damp.

In the world of art, the finest and most elaborately carved work of picture frame-makers is now seen as an art in its own right. And artists have made woodblock prints for centuries. William Caxton and other early

the metal tyre would shrink as it cooled, gripping the whole wheel in a vice-like manner. This was the secret of the old cartwheel's incredible strength.

Wood was even used on the roads they travelled on. There are parts of the old City of London where, under modern tarmac, Victorian wooden paving blocks can still be found driven into the soil. When the Victorians began the massive expansion of Britain's new railway network from the 1830s, the rails rested on solid wooden sleepers; and when they built railways in British colonies all over the world they used local native hardwoods for sleepers: millions of tons of teak beams ended up under locomotives in the Far East.

printers probably used hardwood type rather than metal to create the first printed pages seen in Europe.

In agriculture, ploughs, carts, windmills, stock-proof fences, clogs, hay rakes, pitchforks, scythe handles and other farm implements and numerous farm buildings were made from the cheapest locally available material: wood. And where would the food industry have been without wooden barrels to store everything from herrings to beer and wine? The cooper who made the barrels was a highly skilled craftsman. Even the hoops that bound the barrel staves together could be of wood, harvested from the coppices and split by hand.

Fittingly even the final journey was also made in a wooden box, elm wood being the popular choice for coffins, hence the ancient rhyme, "Elm hateth man / And waiteth".

Elm was traditionally used where the timber was likely to be half submerged in water during its working life, as it lasted far longer than other woods when waterlogged. Hence it was used to make early water pipes, water pumps, riverside pilings, lock gates and timber mooring posts. Other native hardwoods were used along the rivers to make bridges and weirs.

William Caxton probably used hardwood type rather than metal to create the first printed pages seen in Europe

Sustainable, renewable and endlessly useful, wood can be crafted into more or less anything from matchsticks to cathedral roofs. And nothing need ever be wasted – even when its worn, broken, disgarded or just unsuitable to be made into anything, you can always burn it to keep you warm!

LEFT *There are three types of cooper – wet coopers make barrels suitable for holding liquids, dry coopers to hold dry goods, and white coopers make straight staved containers like buckets and butter churns.*

Once the legs have been 'turned' on the pole lathe, the slats of wood for the chair back are steamed and bent to the desired curve, and finished with a drawknife and a spokeshave.

The Mastercrafter

GUY MALLINSON *has turned his cabinet-making skills to the crafting of green wood in a magical woodland workshop in Dorset.*

When Guy Mallinson decided to leave the rat race of London behind him, he set off for deepest Dorset and a seven-acre wood. From here he now runs woodworking courses as well as making extraordinarily beautiful furniture and other items using techniques that are both simple and sustainable.

Guy grew up in London but from his earliest days at school he realised that his passion was for making things from wood. After leaving Bryanston, his school in Dorset where his passion for woodwork was encouraged, he set off for Parnham House where he learned cabinet making under the watchful eye of John Makepeace on one of the best known furniture-making courses in Britain. Then he worked for the furniture designer David Field before attending the Royal College of Art, where he discovered that most of the students, though talented furniture designers, had no hands-on experience of making things themselves.

Guy went on to run a highly successful London furniture company making commissioned pieces for a mix of Arab billionaires and huge multinational corporations, including Disney.

But the lure of the countryside was strong and he eventually decided to kick over the traces and move his own furniture-making business and school to the remote West Dorset village of Holditch, near Forde Abbey. Here he has created a unique camp in the centre of his wood, where wigwam-like tents heated by open fires allow year-round outdoor working, protected from the worst weather.

Though Guy trained as a cabinet maker, he was fascinated by the far more environmentally friendly and sustainable techniques of green wood working. With cabinet-making, timber is dried, sawn into planks and transported hundreds, perhaps thousands, of miles before being used. As much as fifty per cent is discarded. Green wood working, by contrast, uses local timber and low-energy techniques, and almost nothing is wasted. One of the most remarkable things about green wood furniture is that such fine pieces can be produced using relatively few and very basic tools.

> *One of the most remarkable things about green wood furniture is that such fine pieces can be produced using few and very basic tools*

Guy explains the difference between cabinet making and green woodworking, which has become his passion.

'I trained as cabinet-maker and the skills have stood me in good stead but green woodworking has some huge advantages over conventional woodworking – it allows you, for example, to work with the wood using its natural strength. This is less of a factor in cabinet making, where one works with seasoned timber (dry wood) cut into planks.

RIGHT *The burr on a cabinet scraper is used to finish a sycamore spatula on a shaving horse.*

BELOW *Guy uses a roughing out gouge on a billet rotated by the foot-powered pole lathe.*

ABOVE *A collection of mallets of various weights and sizes made from elm, hornbeam and apple.*

'Green wood, which still has its sap and therefore appears almost wet, is so much softer and easier to work. The techniques for working it are also very environmentally friendly, being low-energy and low waste. Our pole lathes rely entirely on human power (in the form of a foot treadle), and much of the rest of the work we do is based around simple gouges and chisels, draw knives and a most marvellous piece of equipment called a shaving horse. This simple device allows you to grip any piece of wood tightly while it is worked on.

'But the process really starts when we select our trees.'

> *The techniques for using green wood are very environmentally friendly and low waste*

Guy tries to make sure that he goes with the forester when timber is being felled because he has very particular requirements.

'We're looking for the straight stem below the branches – branches disrupt the grain and thereby weaken the wood. A good straight stem will give good grain, which is vital to our way of working, using the natural strengths of the timber.

'Once the tree has been cut into lengths and delivered, I stack it in such a way that it doesn't dry out too quickly. When we decide to make something we select a good, suitable log for the job in hand and use a froe to start the process of turning

LEFT *The pole-lathe has the advantage of being simple and portable, an important consideration for many woodland craftsmen.*

BELOW *Carving a sycamore bowl with a gouge and mallet. The mallet is made from dense apple wood that resists splitting.*

ABOVE *Paring end grain with a carving gouge on a totem pole. There are two distinct types of gouge, one shallow, the other deeply hollowed.*

raw wood into a finished spatula, chair leg, skittle or whatever you would like.

'The froe, which is rather like a wedge with a wooden handle fixed at right angles to the blade, is hit with a club (rather like a rough mallet, made by us from hornbeam) to split the chunk of wood. This process of splitting is called cleaving. A side axe is used to get the raw wood close, but not too close, to the shape we want. We then move to the shaving horse and use the drawknife to take the rough block of wood down close to the final shape we need. If the piece needs to be turned, it moves to the pole lathe.

'A cabinet scraper – a metal, half moon-shaped disc with a burred edge – is often used instead of sandpaper for final smoothing.'

> *We don't waste anything: wood that has flaws or knots is put on the fire and keeps us warm*

BELOW *Elm is preferred for seat making as it is best able to stand up to the many processes used in chair-making. This post and rung ash chair has a wych elm woven bark seat.*

It all sounds pretty straightforward but, as Guy explains, only experience can give you the ability to get it right and different people learn at different speeds.

Running courses is a vital part of the mix that allows green wood furniture-making to be a financially viable way of life for Guy. He runs courses for all ages and levels of ability, from those with high skill levels to complete beginners.

Typically, beginners will start by making a simple wooden spatula or a bowl and

progress, if they have the time and talent, to making beautifully crafted chairs that will last several lifetimes, despite being held together without glue, and entirely using the natural tendency of green wood to shrink predictably, to a different degree in each of the three dimensions, to lock the joints.

'Our students have the pleasure of making something and taking it away – whether it's a rolling pin or a garden gate. And we don't waste anything: wood that has flaws or knots is put on the fire and keeps us warm.'

Where high tech will do the job better Guy is not in the least precious. He uses computer software to design 3D objects on his laptop; and where a battery drill will do a better job than a brace and bit, he's happy to use it.

'We're really green but we don't take it to extremes! And though green wood courses are central to what we do, I will never give up accepting commissions for specific pieces – the prospect of designing something new is always enticing!'

ABOVE *Part of the woodland teaching workshop with central fire pits and log walls.*

Marking out the joints is critical to the ultimate strength of the chair. The grain of the legs is carefully orientated as it was on the tree so that the wood will contract predictably. As it dries out, the joints tighten and grip without the need for glue, giving tremendous strength and flexibility to the chair.

The Tradition of Woodwork

From simply gathering firewood to magnificent carvings and enormous constructions, wood is the most valuable and easily worked resource available to man. Its vulnerability to decay means that most ancient woodwork has long since perished but there are enough surviving examples to show an unbroken tradition from the earliest civilisations through to modern times.

Perhaps the most extraordinary early wooden artefact in the world is the great Buddha Hall or daibutsuden in Nara, Japan. Building began in CE728 and what we see today at 57m (187ft) long and 50m (164ft) wide (although subsequently re-built) is a monument to the extraordinary skills of those long-vanished carpenters. The timbers that hold up this vast hall with its gigantic statue of Buddha are the size of mature solid tree trunks, yet they have been shaped and fitted with great delicacy so that, from a distance, the building has lightness and grace. The Horyuji Temple, also at Nara, was completed in the sixth and seventh centuries and is largely unaltered.

ANCIENT WOODWORK

In Europe, timber from very early periods is almost unknown, but a wooden wheel excavated at Wicken Fen in Cambridgeshire shows the skills of workers in the Bronze Age (3300–1200BCE). Many other ancient timbers at this site – mostly used to make walkways across the sodden ground – have also survived, with axe marks that reveal how they were split and shaped.

Nothing remains of Wiltshire's late Neolithic or early Bronze Age wooden versions of Stonehenge, known as woodhenges, except evidence of the deep pits into which massive wooden uprights had been sunk. From these, the careful concentric layout and huge scale of the sites can be understood, but the wood itself has long since disappeared.

Among the most remarkable ancient wooden artefacts, in terms of both their range and quality, are the treasures recovered in the 1920s from the tomb of the Tutankhamen, who reigned 1336–1327BCE.

Magnificently carved and decorated wooden Egyptian coffins had been known from the valley of the kings long before

Tutankhamen's tomb was discovered, and they exist in their thousands and in wonderful condition to this day in museums across the world. Egyptian paintings of the dead on wood also survive, but Tutankhamen's tomb was something very different. Enclosed in it were the young king's gold mask, his gold-covered throne, wooden couches, alabaster vases, various wooden caskets and chests, chairs and stools, wooden chariots and statues, model boats, weapons (including bows) and wooden games.

Wood decays easily and so ancient timber artefacts are rare. We know from the writer Pliny (23–7CE) that the Greeks used cedar wood for many of their carved statues – he specifically mentions a statue of Jupiter carved from cypress wood and erected in Rome in CE97 – but no complete ancient Greek statue in wood survives. Of course, the most remarkable wooden structure, if it existed, would have been the legendary

ABOVE **The Daibutsu-den Hall in Japan is the world's largest wooden structure. 50,000 carpenters, 370,000 metal workers, and 2.18 million labourers worked on its construction.**

LEFT **Great Coxwell Barn is a large tithe barn in Oxfordshire, with a spectacular wooden roof structure built in around 1203.**

ABOVE *Wooden figurine of St Livertin, who was the patron saint of headaches.*

RIGHT *The Oseberg ship was a karvi, a clinker-constructed ship built almost entirely of oak, and measuring 21.4m (70.5ft) long, 5.1m (17ft) wide, and 1.5m (4.9ft) deep, with room for 30 oars.*

Trojan Horse (around 1260BCE)! There is a wooden geared astronomical 'calendar' at Antikythera dated to about 100–150BCE.

Like the Greeks, the Romans traditionally built in stone, and where there was little stone to quarry they were so well organised that they could transport it hundreds or perhaps even thousands of miles. In the old City of London, however, sections of Roman timberwork have been excavated in modern times from the edge of the Thames, where it used to embank the river. It was preserved because the thick, waterlogged mud had such low oxygen levels. Wooden Roman coffins are also known, and wooden writing tablets have survived in large numbers (the centre of each wooden tablet was hollowed out and filled with wax, on to which a stylus was used to scratch the words). The Museum of London has examples of short stretches of hollowed-out wooden Roman pipes that transported water to various places in the city.

SHIPBUILDERS

We know that the Vikings made wonderful wooden carvings in the round as well as producing incised carving and open work. Surviving examples in Scandinavian and British museums suggest that wherever there was wood the Vikings felt they had to decorate it. There is also a great deal of evidence for Viking shipbuilding – particularly from ship burials. The impression left by the 27.4m (90ft) burial ship in the mud at Sutton Hoo in Essex, for example, shows the lines of the timber

> *After the Romans left in the fourth century, Scandinavian invaders introduced their own tradition of timber building*

and even the iron-rust nail marks and as a result archaeologists have been able to gain precise ideas of the woodworking skills that

allowed these remarkable seagoing craft to be built. There are other examples of Viking burial ships, including one at Oseberg in Norway dating from the early ninth century, which is one of the best preserved.

Unique among earlier timber survivals is the Tudor warship *Mary Rose*, now housed in a special museum at Portsmouth. Almost exactly half of the *Mary Rose* – the flagship of Henry VIII's fleet – was perfectly preserved in the mud of the Solent for more than four centuries after she sank in 1545. The wreck yielded huge amounts of information about Tudor shipbuilding techniques as well as thousands of timber items including games, cups, trenchers, boxes, chests, arrows, bows, tools and medical instruments.In rather better repair, Nelson's flagship, *Victory*, also on permanent display today, in Portsmouth, was launched in 1765, and represents the master techniques from the height of European shipbuilding. The craft of the carpenters is evident not just in the construction of the hull and decks but the hundreds of blocks for the rigging and other fittings including the many gun carriages.

BUILDING WITH WOOD

Although the Assyrians, Egyptians, Greeks and Romans typically built in stone, their roofs were certainly held up by timber. The classical pillars that dominate so many old and new buildings throughout Europe and America today are based on ancient Greek pillars that were designed to look like stylised trees.

In Britain, the pre-Roman Celts would have built with local timber, but almost nothing of this survives other than evidence of ancient post holes. After the Romans left in the fourth century, Scandinavian invaders introduced their own tradition of timber building. Archaeological evidence shows that

A woven seat makes a comfortable alternative to the solid windsor chair with a seat carved out using an adze. Wych elm is cut into strips and soaked in water to make it flexible enough to weave. The finished surface is strong and flexible and could almost be mistaken for leather.

ABOVE *Crucks are pairs of curved timber and generally consist of two halves of a tree trunk, as seen in this half timbered cottage in Didbrook, Gloucestershire. Crucks are regarded as one of the earliest types of timber frame.*

a remarkably solid box frame, which was inherently rigid. It was a momentous change.

A slightly earlier building style that survives in a number of cottages and smaller houses (particularly in Worcestershire and Herefordshire) is the cruck frame. Here massive pairs of curving oak timbers (the cruck) were used in an A-shape to make each end of the house, and then joined together by subsidiary timbers.

Britain is particularly fortunate in having

> *Medieval barns, some as lofty as cathedrals, have survived in some numbers in Britain*

a large number of early timber buildings. It also has some of the finest museums in the world and the collecting instincts of earlier generations have ensured that they contain many of the rarest and most beautiful wooden items in the world.

In Suffolk, a county that traditionally built in local oak, huge numbers of wonderful timber-framed buildings survive, but among the finest is the Tudor Guildhall at Lavenham, which was completed in 1529. The Guildhall was built with far more timber than it needed to be structurally sound, the reason being that the powerful guilds that commissioned the building wanted it to show off their wealth. But the importance of Lavenham lies also in its display of the medieval woodworker's art in dozens of surviving buildings, and in a pattern of streets and buildings that is, in essence, medieval.

Hundreds of small churches up and down the country boast splendid medieval Tudor or later roofs, screens, choir stalls and pulpits. Among the least altered is the little chapel of St Michael near Lechlade in Gloucestershire. Here the intricately

they made their buildings rigid by pushing wall posts directly into the earth. This is a sure way of reducing the lifespan of the building, as water quickly rots the bottoms of the posts.

In houses and barns the big change in Europe came with box framing: instead of bracing the timber structure by inserting uprights into the ground, the uprights were inserted into a wallplate or sill beam running along the ground or along a rubble course. Roof timbers were also attached to the uprights and crossing timbers using a new elaborate pegged joint that created carved screen and other woodwork can be seen in a church that escaped those zealous Victorian restorers who, in fact, destroyed a great deal of medieval work in their zest for 'improvement'.

One of the marvels of late medieval Europe (and this was even recognised at the time) was Master Harland's completion in 1400 of the hammerbeam roof that still survives at Westminster Hall in London. Here, in order to create a sense of height and space in the centre of the hall, the tie beams (which normally run from wall to wall) have been cut short on each side near the walls. These short remaining beams, supported by curved wooden braces, are known as the hammerbeams. Above the short beams and supported by them rise massive timbers that curve across the height of the roof before descending to the matching hammerbeams extending from the walls on the other side of the hall.

Medieval barns, some as lofty as cathedrals, have survived in some numbers in Britain and among the finest are Middle Littleton tithe barn near Evesham in Worcestershire, built in the 1200s, and the slightly later tithe barn at Bredon near Tewkesbury, Gloucestershire. Both are owned or administered by the National Trust and show the medieval timber roof builder's craft at its finest.

The Weald and Downland Museum in Sussex has a splendid collection early timber-framed buildings, as well as carts and carriages that show how brilliantly wood was once used to make the vehicles that kept Britain moving – and fed. At the top end of the social scale, the best example of the coachbuilder's art survives at the Royal Mews in London: the Irish state coach is a masterpiece of gilded wood, carved into intricate and elaborate decorative designs.

To see how craftsmen made the intricate cogs, wheels and other mechanisms for watermills and windmills you can visit the remarkable water mill on the Thames at Mapledurham, Oxfordshire, where stone-ground flour is still being produced.

WOOD CARVING AND FURNITURE MAKING

Wooden statues of saints – carved using gouges and chisels manipulated with wooden mallets – filled the Catholic churches of Europe from their earliest foundation. These were almost always painted and they were made in miniature for private worship and in much larger sizes for public church worship. In England probably as much as 99 per cent of this art was destroyed during the Reformation in the sixteenth century but Europe's medieval churches still contain

BELOW *Lavenham Guildhall is a timber-framed Tudor building in the heart of the well preserved medieval village of Lavenham, Suffolk.*

many examples that show the skill of the woodcarver and give us a tantalising glimpse of the wealth of treasures that have been lost.

Among the finest examples of late medieval wood carving are the screen at St Helen Ranworth, Norfolk, and the choir stalls at Salisbury Cathedral. But perhaps rarest of all is the wooden church at Greensted near Ongar in Essex. Here the original split-oak walls can still be seen. They date from the eighth or ninth century.

The magnificent carved oak front of Sir Paul Pindar's Jacobean house still exists in the Victoria and Albert Museum in London, for example, along with the Great Bed of Ware. It was probably made by the carpenter Jonas Fosbrooke in the last quarter of the sixteenth century. Measuring 3m by 3.3m (10ft by 11ft), it is made using marquetry technique, which is specifically mentioned in Shakespeare's comedy *Twelfth Night*.

Perhaps the most significant carved piece of wooden furniture in Britain is the high-backed gothic-style Coronation Chair at Westminster Abbey. Carved from oak in 1301 by a carpenter known only as Master Walter,

{ *Power tools transformed the process of cutting, planing and fitting* }

it has been subject to numerous repairs over the centuries, but every English monarch since 1308 has been crowned on this chair.

In furniture, the medieval system of joining wood using simple slotted joints or pegs driven into aligned holes gradually gave way to mortise and tenon joints and dovetail joints that, when glued, produced a strong bond, enabling thinner timber to be used. Whereas medieval chests used thick planks, 18th century chests of drawers were built with drawer sides that could be only a quarter of an inch thick.

Cabinet-making, as skilled furniture-making came to be known, had developed into a style of work based on carcase making and fine finishing. By then fine furniture was being decorated with superb veneers that might show hunting or religious scenes or geometric patterns, and there was a wider choice of woods. In Britain oak, or for rare items walnut, had remained the timber of choice until the rise of the merchant classes in the eighteenth century. The increase in trade meant that larger amounts of new timber began to be imported. For example, mahogany was being imported from Jamaica and other Caribbean islands owned at that time by the British. It became hugely fashionable in furniture making for its beautiful colour, its strength and because it was resistant to woodworm.

Cheaper domestic timber artefacts began to be made with imported softwoods at this time. As the Industrial Revolution transformed the world of manufacturing, water power, steam and (much later) diesel and electric power meant that sawmills could churn out finished timber at a rate undreamt of in earlier epochs. Power tools transformed the process of cutting, planing and fitting. Mass production made its presence felt.

At the end of the nineteenth century the Arts and Crafts movement, spearheaded by

William Morris (1834–1896), represented a reaction against the factory-made and an attempt to revive locally-produced handmade furniture and other items. But that new tradition declined in the 1920s because of the expense of producing hand-crafted products. The designs of the Arts and Crafts, Art Nouveau and Art Deco movements could be reproduced in factory-made furniture and so local craft-based production began to fade once again.

The twentieth century saw woodworking change beyond all recognition with the use of laminated chipboard and multi-density fibreboard (MDF) furniture in the production of elaborate yet cheap furniture, a process that eventually led to the post-World War II desire for the ultra modern: plastics made in bright colours, steel and glass. Victorian and earlier timber furniture became deeply unfashionable and many fine pieces were destroyed. By the 1980s, as the young bought older terraced houses and became interested in the past once again, there was a revival of interest in restoration and original features. In older houses, large structural beams that had been covered up with plaster in the nineteenth and early twentieth centuries were uncovered again, polished and proudly displayed.

Today the wheel has turned again, and we long for handmade wooden furniture, boats, barrels and other traditional things that are made to last and that make the best of locally available, environmentally friendly materials transformed by the hands of a master craftsman.

> *In Britain oak had remained the timber of choice until the rise of the merchant classes in the eighteenth century*

GLASS MAKING

The Craft of Glass Making

There is something hypnotic about the craft of glass blowing – watching as a substance that can be both unforgiving and fragile in its hardened state becomes so malleable under intense heat that it can be blown like a rubber balloon into a globe, and shaped into almost anything. There is also infinite scope for colouring what is naturally a clear or faintly tinged raw material, creating the rainbow magic of another craft: stained glass.

Glass is so much a part of our everyday lives now that it is difficult to imagine a time when the world had to do without it. Imagine no windows, no spectacles, drinking glasses or bottles, no television, no light bulbs.

Most of all we take bottles and drinking glasses for granted – glass has long been ideal for these domestic items because it does not absorb smells and flavours. Even the smell of strong liquids left for years in a bottle can be quickly removed and the bottle used for something else.

Modern science is unimaginable without glass laboratory dishes, tubes and pipettes. And of course highly polished and accurately shaped glass is essential in the manufacture of microscopes – and telescopes that can see deep into space. Glass fibre is widely used in everything from boat building to pipes, safety equipment and insulation and has wide applications in medicine, science and telecommunications. The ultimate in glass fibre development is the fibre optic cable which has transformed our communications systems. In this new technology, glass is formed into fibres that are only micrometres in diameter.

On the home front, before there were glazed windows, light was admitted into houses and churches through narrow slits, or openings with wooden shutters. Even the rich could not afford much window glass in medieval times; for example, Stokesay Castle in Shropshire, dating from the twelfth century and which survives today almost unaltered, was built for a local magnate but had to have basic wooden shutters that could be closed to keep out the elements. Once window glass became more widely

available it became something of a status symbol. Most famously Hardwick Hall in Derbyshire, now owned by the National Trust but built for one of England's richest Elizabethan women, Bess of Hardwick, was deliberately designed with the maximum number and size of windows in order to impress her neighbours. The development of glass sheets for window panes was a major step in architecture and today skyscrapers are often designed with entire sheet-glass walls to create spectacular life-reflecting mirrors on a huge scale. Glass has always had a special relationship with light.

THE RAW MATERIAL

Obsidian is a rare thing: a natural volcanic glass. Rich in silica, it forms when lava solidifies rapidly without crystallisation and it was used in prehistoric times for arrow heads and other weapons: its edges can be made as sharp as flint.

ABOVE *Volcanic glass is unstable and tends to change spontaneously. Geologically, ancient glass is very rare, and most glassy rocks are more than 65.5 million years old.*

LEFT *The single most common use for industrial sand is glass making. Glass sand requires a high level of silica; the presence of other elements such as iron oxide creates visible impurities that blight its transparency.*

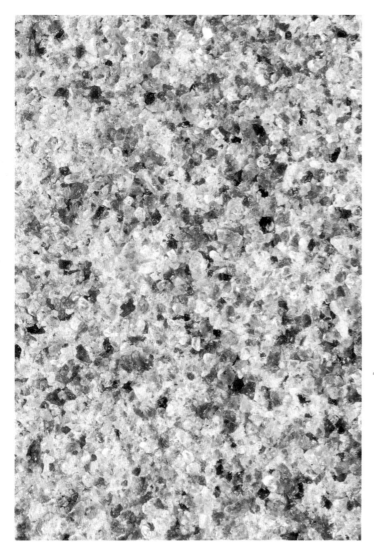

ABOVE *Glass can be recycled indefinitely because its structure does not deteriorate when reprocessed. It can then be used to make bottles and jars, 'processed sand' (finely ground glass used in golf course bunkers), and 'glassphalt' for road surfacing.*

calcium anyway (from shells of long-defunct marine creatures) and so, in theory, if you manage to heat beach sand to such a high temperature that it melts, you can make glass – and if you throw in some soda you won't have to heat it to such an extreme temperature to fuse the ingredients. The bulk of world glass production today is soda-lime glass.

The basic raw materials for glass are easily come by. Almost forty per cent of the world's annual production of more than ninety-four million tons of industrial sand is used to make glass. In addition, as much as thirty-five percent of glass is made by melting down crushed recycled glass, known as cullet.

> *Almost forty percent of the world's annual production of more than ninety-four million tons of industrial sand is used to make glass*

As for soda, something in the region of one million tons of sodium carbonate is produced and sold in the UK each year, and ninety percent of it goes to the glass-making industry. Historically, soda ash (the common name for anhydrous sodium carbonate) was obtained from the ashes of sodium-rich plants, especially those known as glasswort or saltwort, or in the form of natron (hydrated sodium carbonate found on some dried-out sodium-rich saline lake beds, especially in ancient times in Egypt). Sodium carbonate can be made industrially from sea salt mixed with crushed limestone and other agents. Both are mined throughout the world, but in the UK salt is mined only in Cheshire, where it has been extracted at least since Roman times.

A higher content of soda ash ensures that the molten glass hardens slowly, making

The earliest 'manufactured' glass was melted quartz. Glass is formed when quartz, or silica (silicon dioxide), is melted and then cooled. In practice, because silica has such a high melting point – around 1710°C (3110°F) – most types of glass were and are created from silica combined with soda (sodium carbonate) as a 'flux', which lowers the melting point considerably and makes big savings on furnace fuel. But the soda makes the glass soft and to some degree soluble, so calcium carbonate (limestone) or some other ingredient was added as a 'stabiliser'.

Silica is the dominant component in sand grains. Beach sand usually contains

RIGHT *To prepare a handle the craftsman guides the molten crystal to the jug, keeping it in line with the spout. As the crystal cools, it is gently moulded into an arc.*

the task of glass blowers simpler by giving them more time to work on the material before it sets. The addition of potash as flux to lower the melting point gives a very hard glass that hardens quickly – not so good for glass blowers but durable. Potash is produced from wood ashes left after burning broadleaf trees or potassium-rich plants, such as bracken. Potash also occurs as a rock mineral and can be mined, typically as a major agricultural fertiliser: in the UK it comes from just one mine, situated in North Yorkshire, where the mine shafts descend to a seam that runs more than five miles off shore deep under the North Sea.

Another flux is lead oxide, the key ingredient in the making of sparkling lead glass. The oxide melts easily; the glass is soft enough to work at lower temperatures (especially useful for complex cutting and faceting) and has a stunning brilliance. Lead oxide is readily obtained by smelting lead ore, such as galena.

There are other substances that can be added, including those that colour or clarify the glass, or reduce the bubbles in it, or give it special qualities like heat resistance (for example, borosilicate glass, familiar in the form of Pyrex ovenware) or impact resistance (toughened glass), and in fibre optics a whole range of elements, such as titanium, germanium, erbium, boron and aluminium, can be added to silica glass to vary its properties. Non-silica fluoride and phosphate glasses are also used in fibre optics, but silica-based glass (especially soda-lime) remains by far the most common type of commercially produced glass for all kinds of applications.

RIGHT *The exact amount of molten glass should be gathered on the blowing iron to suit the job in hand. The molten glass collects at the end of the iron, and from then on the 'treacly gob' can be kept on the nose only by constant rotation.*

HOW GLASS MAKERS WORK

Although factory-made glass techniques and machinery would baffle an ancient glass maker, the craft side of glass working is more or less unchanged in more than two thousand years. The decorative use of glass is limited only by imagination.

While it is still hot enough to be malleable, glass can be shaped by means of blowing, moulding or pressing. It is then cooled so that the glass 'sets' in the desired shape. Regulation of the temperature of the material at different stages is a crucial part of all glass working. In glass blowing, for example, there are typically three furnaces. In order of decreasing heat, the first and hottest furnace is where a crucible of molten glass is maintained. The second, the 'glory hole', is where an article is reheated between various working stages. The third is the annealer, or lehr, a tunnel in which the final glass object is cooled slowly over anything from a few hours to a few days. This controlled slow cooling is important to avoid cracking or shattering.

Sophisticated furnaces are used today, and they can produce large amounts of molten glass which are manipulated rapidly and extremely accurately by automated machines, but the basic role they play in melting raw glass is no different from that played by ancient furnaces.

Coloured glass

To create glass of different colours the traditional glass maker added various metal compounds (usually oxides) – iron for pale aqua, cobalt for deep royal blue, iron and sulphur for amber, manganese for purple, copper for blue and green, lead for dark green, copper and lead for opaque red to brown, antimony for white, antimony and lead for yellow, and gold chloride for 'cranberry' or gold ruby glass.

ABOVE *Roman craftsmen developed the art of millefiori, a type of ornament still made today by embedding pieces of coloured glass rods in clear glass to create floral designs.*

A distinct glass making technique known as murrine (named for the Venetian island of Murano) involved stretching molten glass of different colours into rods of different sizes, layering the rods in patterns, fusing them together and then cooling and slicing across these 'canes' to reveal identically repeating patterns. The famous millefiori ('thousand flowers') pattern is a variation of this technique.

Stained glass

'Stained' glass is glass that has been coloured by the addition of various metallic oxides during the glass making process, or glass that has been superficially painted and the colour then fused to the glass in a kiln. Stained glass makers use a range of decorative techniques, many of them ancient, to colour their glass. These include adding several layers of paint and then scratching a design

{ *Controlled slow cooling is important to avoid cracking or shattering* }

on and through them. One interesting technique is silver staining, a technique that involves painting silver nitrate on the back of the glass to create a gold tint.

Stained glass makers begin with a template of the window or space they intend to fill. A small sample design, called a vidimus (Latin for 'we have seen'), is made for the client, followed by a full-scale drawing or 'cartoon' showing the detailed design for every light, or opening, in the window. A big window in a cathedral might have many lights and the skill of the Stained glass maker is to design these so that they become, in the completed window, a single unified design. The position of the lead that holds each piece of stained glass in place is an intrinsic part of the design.

> *Glassworkers used heat to melt quartz and then shaped the molten material over a simple compressed sand mould*

Small pieces of coloured glass, often hand-blown in the same workshop, are carefully cut to shape and fitted into the designed pattern or picture. The glass pieces are held together by strips of lead (the method is also seen in plain-glass leaded lights in old cottage windows) to form a stained-glass window or panel. Thus stained-glass workers need to work with lead as well as glass, though today copper foil is often used instead of lead. Like their medieval counterparts many modern stained glass makers create their own lead cames using molten lead poured into suitable moulds.

As each piece of glass is selected it is 'grozed' to ensure a perfect fit (a grozing tool trims small amounts of material from the edge of each piece of glass) and then fitted into the lead framework. All the lead is soldered and the glass made tight using putty pressed between glass and lead.

Glass blowing

When the craft of glass-forming first evolved, glass workers used heat to melt quartz and then shaped the molten material over a simple compressed sand mould. This process of casting glass is popular with modern glass artists and the ancient technique is also still used to make more functional objects, though the modern moulds may be made from graphite or metal.

It was not until some 2,000 years ago that the technique of glass blowing rather than casting was first used to create hollow vessels. From blowing simple bowls and pots glass makers learned to attach handles and spouts, and to add complex decoration. Glass blowing quickly became the almost universal method of forming glass objects – including flat glass for windows. Glass blowing remains central to craft glasswork.

There are two main methods of glass blowing. In free blowing, the glass is simply blown into the air and shaped during the blow. In mould blowing, it is free blown into roughly the shape and size of the final article and then put into a mould for the final touches.

Most important of the glass blower's tools is the blowpipe or blow iron which, in its standard form, is made today from stainless steel and measures roughly 127cm (50in) long and around 2½cm (1in) in diameter. In ancient times, before metalworking was known, blowpipes or 'mouthblowers' were made of clay.

The basic process for blowing a glass object follows a well established pattern. For free blowing, the heated tip of the blowpipe is dipped into a pot of molten glass and rolled to gather a blob of a size appropriate to the article that is being made. This 'gather' adheres to the end of the pipe and is then 'marvered' (rolled on a marble, iron or steel slab) to form a bubble known

as the 'parison'. The blower manipulates the parison by reheating it and blowing air into it in short puffs, constantly rotating it to counteract gravity and constantly reheating to keep it pliable, until the glass is the right size and shape. Spoon-shaped, water-soaked wooden blocks are used during the blow to help in the shaping, and flat wooden or graphite paddles are used to shape flat areas, for example the base of a jug or vase.

When the glass has been inflated to its basic shape various tools are used to

BELOW *Blowing needs unerring judgement of temperature and pressure in order to produce vessels of a consistent size and thickness. The tube has to be warmed before its nose is lowered into molten glass.*

complete the desired piece – adding a handle here or a spout there and finally cutting the glass from the tube. Glass-cutting clippers or shears are used to trim excess molten glass and to cut and shape the more intricate parts of whatever is being blown. Tongs and pliers are used to hand-form red-hot glass. Glass

> *A tell-tale dimple on the bottom of a handmade object shows where the pontil was once attached*

maker's tweezers are vital for holding, sculpting, twisting and generally shaping the object. Modern glass blowers also use glass knives or scorers to cut rods of glass.

For an open-necked vessel, a solid metal rod known as a pontil is attached to the base of the vessel while the glass is still hot; the article can then be cut free from the blowpipe and the neck opening left by the blowpipe can be worked to its final shape while the blower uses the pontil to hold the piece. Jacks – tools with two metal blades joined at one end by a handle – are used to form the mouths of open vessels. The size of the jack's gape can be varied by the glass blower. Metal jacks can leave marks on the glass so in certain circumstances wooden jacks, or more modern graphite versions, are used. A tell-tale dimple on the bottom of a handmade object shows where the pontil was once attached.

In mould blowing, the partly free-blown article is transferred to a wetted wooden or a metal mould and blown to its final shape. In a wooden mould, steam cushions the glass from touching the wood, but in a metal mould contact is part of the process: the sides of a metal mould might have indentations or decorations that imitate cut-glass designs. When the cooled glass is removed from the mould it will have taken on the design without the need for cutting.

Lampwork

Lampworkers use hot flames to work glass rods and tubes into decorative beads, glass sculptures (a modern development of the craft) and, more practically, laboratory glassware, including botanical and animal 'model' structures. In contrast to glass blowing, lampworkers usually manipulate their heated glass with tools and gravity rather than by inflation with a blowpipe, but otherwise many of the tools are similar for both crafts.

Traditionally lampworkers used oil lamps, intensifying the flame with bellows or their own breath, but today they use propane or natural gas (or butane) pumped with oxygen; the craft is now also called flameworking or torchworking. They work with soda-lime 'soft' glass or with the more expensive borosilicate 'hard' glass, and sometimes lead glass. Coloured glass is essential for most decorative work.

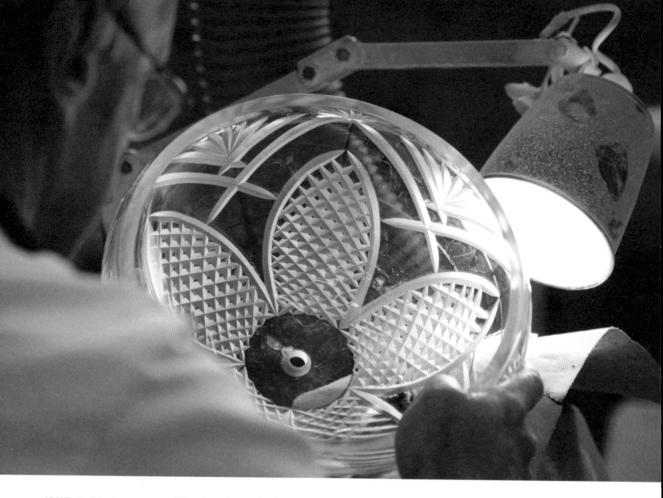

ABOVE *Working to a pattern marked on the glass, the glass cutter presents the object to a power driven, diamond edge wheel. The depth and angle of each cut is critical to release reflections and light.*

RIGHT *After it has been cut, the glassware is dipped in acid to restore the brilliance of the cut surfaces.*

The glass is acquired in pre-formed rods, or sheet glass is cut into strips. It is also possible to buy glass 'frit' or powdered particles as surface decoration on beads. For lampworked beads, the basic steps are to prepare the mandrel (a kind of fine metal rod) by dipping it into a clay solution, heating glass rods in the flame and winding the heated glass on to the mandrel. The beads are then shaped with a combination of heat, gravity, tools and presses before decorating them and finally heating them again to anneal the glass, releasing any inherent stresses that would cause it to crack or shatter. Further work can be carried out when the beads are cold, such as sanding, faceting, polishing or etching.

Glass decorating

Etching decorative designs onto glass involves covering the glass with wax or paraffin and cutting the lines of the design into the wax. The glass is then dipped in acid and the corrosive action of the acid etches the design into the glass surface – but only through the fine lines that expose the glass.

Etching is often combined with enamelling and engraving to create detailed and very beautiful effects. Enamelling involves coating one surface of the glass with mineral pigments and then heating until pigment and glass fuse.

Glass engravers hold glass against an abrasive wheel which, in the hands of a skilled operator, can produce an astonishing range of special decorative effects. Alternatively the engraver may use a tool tipped with diamond or tungsten carbide to scratch lines in the glass. Tapping this tool on the surface of the glass produces an entirely different stippled effect. Modern techniques of glass engraving include using lasers to do the cutting.

For several centuries glass has been cut and faceted to imitate – often very successfully – cut diamonds and other precious stones. The glass cutter holds the item to be decorated against a copper wheel that spins rapidly while running through a liquid containing an abrasive. In practised hands the facets (flat surfaces ground into the main body of the glass) have a dazzlingly bright ability to reflect light – just as multi-faceted cuts on a diamond create the ultimate sparkle effect.

Glass fusing encompasses slumping (firing at relatively low temperatures), tack fusing (firing at higher temperatures) and full fusing (which demands the highest temperatures of all). The most commonly adopted fusing technique in use today is stacking, where thin sheets of differently coloured glass are stacked one on top of the other and then heated till they meld together. Different effects can be achieved by controlling the kiln temperature.

Etching is often combined with enamelling and engraving to create detailed and very beautiful effects

Glass lettering involves the use of dry zinc mixed with mucilage (a thick glutinous plant derivative) and then applied by brush in a range of colours to the surface of the glass.

One of the most beautiful of all decorative glass techniques is gilding – the application of gold leaf on the back or inside surface of the glass. The gilding is ultimately viewed through the glass which greatly adds to the lustre of the design. The skill comes in adding the design while working back to front (so that the design appears the right way round when viewed).

BELOW *When fused glass, which is heated in a kiln, becomes soft enough, layers of different colour fuse together.*

The Mastercrafter

SOPHIE LISTER
HUSSAIN

*creates highly
individual stained
glass designs for
public and private
clients and has
found the medium
the ideal outlet for
her creativity.*

The art of stained glass making dates back at least to medieval times. It combines a range of craft skills with the skills of the painter. To many it evokes ancient church windows, but it is actually an important artistic discipline that has survived throughout the centuries intact and largely unchanged, though the colours and designs used by stained glass artists today would astonish and perhaps even delight their medieval counterparts.

Sophie Lister Hussain is a talented stained glass artist who grew up on the Isle of Anglesey, off the coast of North Wales, which was a primary influence in her early artistic development.

'My earliest memories are of my grandmother. She taught me to knit and to sew and and the combining of a multitude of different materials. She also instilled in me the self discipline to strive to do my very best with anything I made.'

This creativity inspired Sophie early on, so that when she left school she was determined to go to Art college, but making a decision about which precise media to study was not quite so straightforward.

'I found a course studying glass and ceramics at Wrexham College of Art in North Wales and I really liked the sound of it, but I had I had no relevant experience of glass working. In order to secure a last minute place on the course I persuaded the course tutor, Mel Harris, to interview me. I arrived with a portfolio of fashion drawings, landscape drawings and paintings, clothes I had made, cloth that I had dyed and an array of large and small abstract pots.'

Once on the course, Sophie realised that this was something that really worked for her. She felt that she'd found her artistic home.

'It was a great course, because it taught me the disciplines of how to cut glass, and cutline glass, how to think in glass, the way large scale colours worked and how to use them. We also learned technical skills such as sand-blasting, surface decoration, kiln work and hydrofluoric acid-etching. We learned how art and architecture could work together.

One project involved us designing glass for Wrexham swimming pool, which meant you were working on something that would be seen out there in the real world

'One specific design proposal was for the main window overlooking the pool at Wrexham Swimming Pool. This was my first design project and was judged by renowned stained glass artist Eugene Politti.

'In my final year I designed a window for a church just outside Oswestry in Shropshire – my design was of alpha and omega and I did it in really bright colours and in handmade double-plated English glass. Everyone on the course had to come up with a design, but my design won, which was a brilliant boost for me. I remember I etched the design into the glass using hydrofluoric acid.'

ABOVE *Lining up a joint, using the Don Carlos leading knife and the oyster knife to position the leads so that they are square, ready to solder.*

RIGHT *Sophie prefers to use a gas soldering iron as she finds it gives a constant heat, is reliable and faster than electric irons.*

After that success there was no looking back, and Sophie went on to come joint first in the Stevens Architectural Glass competition to design a commemorative window for Laurence Olivier.

'That was a really interesting project,' she recalls. 'It was a competition run by the Worshipful Company of Glaziers. My design, which incorporated a line drawing of the National Theatre, won and, although the window was never made, it was great to feel that my design had really stood out.'

Winning the first prize also opened up her first real working experience within a major stained glass studio, as she was offered a work placement during the following summer months at the prestigious firm of Goddard and Gibbs.

After leaving Wrexham College, Sophie studied Two- and Three-Dimensional Glass and Ceramics at Sunderland University.

'It was a three-year course that gave me the time to carry on working for Goddard & Gibbs every summer. After finishing at Sunderland I worked for G & G for a year and then took the plunge and went freelance, working for a number of other studios – I worked for some of the great names in stained glass making, including Alf Fisher and Bernard Becker, Deborah Coombs and Ginger Ferrell.'

Sophie insists that when it comes to glass there is inevitably more to learn, which is why she is always keen to meet and work with other artists. It wasn't until 2000 that she felt fully confident that she knew enough to start completely on her own.

'I lived on a traditional narrow boat in West London and built a make-shift little lean-to studio at the side of the boat. I managed to get lots of interesting work, often making bespoke stained glass windows, and it taught me the rudimentaries and gave me the skill base for all the work I've made since.'

The process of working through a commission with the client is something that Sophie likes to oversee carefully from the outset.

'You begin by meeting the client and discussing various ideas. You might talk to them on numerous occasions to hone details down to the final design, until they are satisfied. Some clients are quite sure of what they want, while others will largely leave it up to me.'

She still makes stained glass for small private houses, but she also works on big public commissions.

'A recent commission was a window for the Chapel at St Saviour's and St Olave's School in London. They asked me to design two windows incorporating the school motto in glass.'

After this commission Sophie was approached to make a centenary glass and mosaic window for the school's stairwell. This was officially opened by Queen Elizabeth II.

Sophie is fascinated by all types of glass work, but especially her own specialism of stained glass.

'The majority of my work is stained glass. It's always etched with acid or painted with kiln firing paints, silver stained or surface decorated by sandblasting stencil work; a combination of any or all of these techniques can give a detailed and rich texture to the surface of glass. Sandblasting gives glass a frosted appearance, and can be used to shade areas of clear glass; painting can be done in many different colours straight on

ABOVE *Soldering a joint with the gas iron.*

BELOW *Preparing lead in the correct position for soldering.*

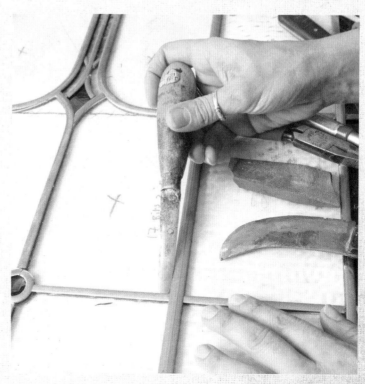

> *I always try to push the boundaries even beyond my own experience*

to the glass; and etching produces a range of interesting effects, melting away the surface of unmasked glass.

'After the client is happy with the design, the making of the glass follows the same procedure each time. First I measure the window frame – this has to be done accurately. The rebate, sight size, full making size, tight size and mullions all need to be accounted for, support bars, tie wires, internal steel cored lead, saddle leads, thread leads, the list is endless.

BELOW *The glass maker's toolkit: various knives, a glass cutter, pliers, a hammer and horseshoe nails and a soldering iron.*

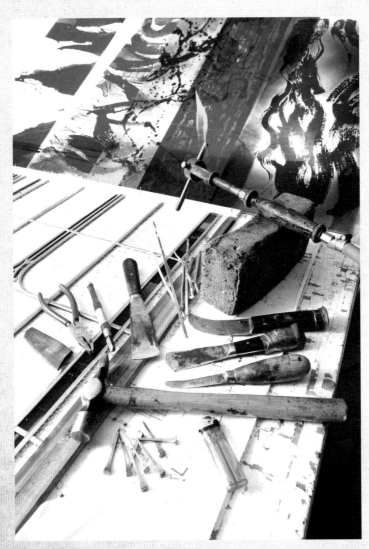

'Once they have been approved, designs are enlarged to a full sized working drawing. Any indication of glass paint, silver stain and etching is marked, drawn to scale and even sketched on to the cartoon.

'A cut line drawing is taken from the cartoon, which shows each and every piece of glass, the lines indicate the heart of all the leads, a line that glass cutters know should not to be crossed.

'When the glass pieces are ready you "lead it up" – start fixing all the pieces into their positions using a lead knife, pliers and horseshoe nails.'

Stained glass tools wear into the hands of the maker, and it takes time to become accustomed to a new tool. Glass painting brushes are especially hard to break in and require hours of work to become effective and supple.

By the time that the glass is fitted into the leads, the windows soldered and cemented, the old frame amended to fit again, or the new frame securely installed into the building, then the finished glass can finally be installed into the frame.

For Sophie it is not technique but personality, drive and enthusiasm that really transforms a stained-glass window into something unique and important.

ABOVE *Soldering the border of a design with the gas iron, using lead tin solder.*

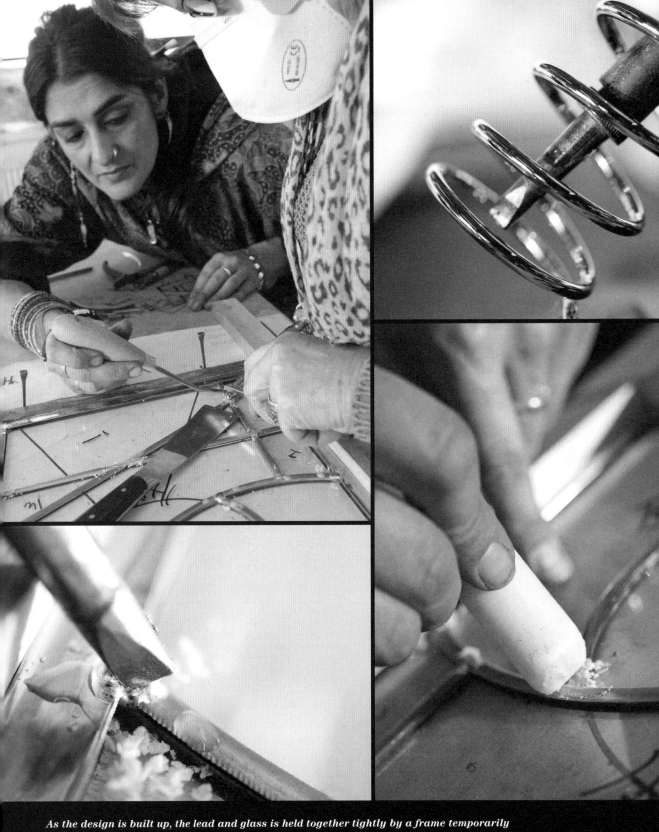

As the design is built up, the lead and glass is held together tightly by a frame temporarily nailed up against it with horseshoe nails. The joints in the leading are prepared with

The Tradition of Glass Making

The elements that make glass are hidden in grains of sand, and the discovery that molten sand could put a shiny glaze on clay beads was an accidental one that would lead, ultimately, to skyscrapers clad from top to bottom with glass. The tradition of moulding molten glass into beads and vessels took a dramatic leap some 2,000 years ago when someone put a blob of molten glass on the end of a hollow tube and puffed: the art of glass blowing was born.

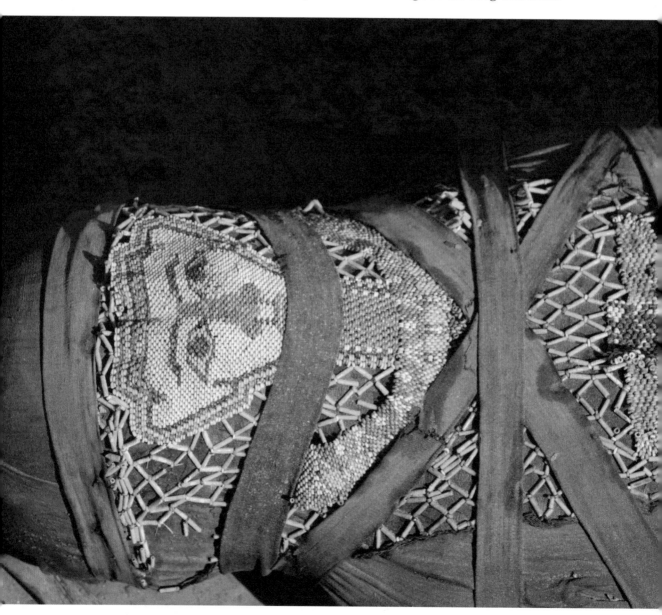

Though the basic techniques for craft glass making have changed little over the centuries, industrial processes have enabled glass to be produced cheaply and in vast quantities in more recent times.

The earliest glass in the form of melted quartz crystals was used to coat pottery beads and small statues. Within a few generations melted quartz was being shaped around various moulds, the earliest probably being clay: a sandy clay core was moulded over the end of a metal rod in the shape of a vessel; the rod was dipped into molten glass and rotated rapidly to coat the core.

Making beads was one of the earliest applications of glass and the ancient Egyptians took their glass bead-making seriously. A few glass beads made around 4,500 years ago have been found from the Old Kingdom. But first the Egyptians invented what is now known as Egyptian faience (not the same as tin-glazed clay pottery faience). This was a paste based on crushed quartz with lime and other alkalis (usually potash) given a surface vitrification (i.e. a glass coating or glaze) by firing which, because of the presence of copper, was usually a bright turquoise and therefore a good substitute for semi-precious stones. Faience was an artificial material which in

its earliest form was worked by means of modelling, scraping and grinding when it was cold, like stone, with the bead threading holes being drilled by hand. In later dynasties, faience was worked when it was still pliable and the paste was modelled or pressed into clay moulds before firing.

By around 2300BCE all-glass beads were being made in Mesopotamia and the Caucasus by methods such as core-forming or winding: warm malleable glass was wound around a clay-wrapped wire to form the bead hole and then decorated in various ways. There was even a bead-making industry in Britain by 1900BCE. By 1500BCE, mosaic beads were being created by fusing bundles of thin glass rods.

Glass manufacture in any quantity only really got going in ancient Egypt during the New Kingdom period (1150–1070BCE), and skills developed rapidly in creating often very colourful and quite elaborate functional and decorative glass vessels. By 300BCE glass engravers were already at work using wheel-cutting techniques to engrave brown and green glass bowls.

> { *Making beads was one of the earliest applications of glass* }

FAR LEFT *A beaded faience – a glazed non-clay ceramic material or silica, composed of crushed quartz – covers the body of a mummy that was discovered at the ancient burial site of Saqqara, Egypt.*

LEFT *Ancient Egyptian glass was regarded as artificial semi-precious stone. This rare glass was excavated from an an ancient cargo which sunk more than 1,000 years ago in the Java Sea.*

BELOW *Fragments of decorative mosaic glass made in Egypt during the Ptolemaic or Roman periods, approximately 332BCE–200CE.*

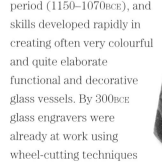

Glass blowing was arguably the greatest development in the long history of glass making. Invented around 50CE, probably in Syria or Palestine, it enabled glass artefacts to be produced faster, more cheaply and in more complex designs than ever before.

Increasingly beautiful decorative techniques developed over the ensuing centuries, including enamelling. The Romans were highly skilled glass enamellers: using enamel paint they could add detailed and colourful designs to the surface of the glass that was then fixed by heating.

Around the year 1000CE the difficulty and expense of importing soda (usually from Egypt) to create soda glass – then the most commonly made glass in Europe – led to a major change in materials: it was discovered that potash, which could be cheaply produced from burned trees, was a good replacement for soda. While Italy continued the tradition of making soda glass,

*ABOVE **This bowl would have been made in a glasshouse in the eastern provinces of the Roman Empire, between 50–75CE. Painted decoration on glass that has survived from this period is likely to have been enamelled – patterns painted onto cold glass would have disappeared.***

*RIGHT **Crown glass was one of the most common processes for making glass for windows up until the nineteenth century.***

> *The Romans were highly skilled glass enamellers: using enamel paint they could add detailed and colourful designs*

northern European countries shifted to the new potash glass.

Although the Romans had cast-glass window panes in their most luxurious villas, they didn't admit much light. For centuries, flat window glass was made by glass blowing. First came broad sheet (known examples in England date from the thirteenth century), in which molten glass was blown into an elongated balloon shape, the ends cut off and the resulting still-hot cylinder was split with shears and flattened on an iron plate, full of imperfections and small in size, and used in leaded lights. Even though these panes were too small to admit much light they did at least establish the idea of windows as real possibilities. Small coloured panes began to be used in churches and over succeeding centuries the magnificent tradition of stained glass windows spread and developed across Europe.

Another of the earliest types was crown glass, first produced in France in 1330: molten glass was blown into a balloon shape, the blowpipe was removed, a pontile rod was attached to the other end of the balloon and the glass was spun rapidly to form a disc, or it was blown into a hollow container and spun rapidly on a revolving table to flatten the glass by centrifugal force. This created a round, flat sheet, which could be trimmed into a rectangle, but at the centre a thicker 'bulls-eye' area distorted views through the glass and usually needed to be ground down or cut away for other purposes.

The great masters of glass blowing were the Venetians and Venice is still renowned as a centre of glass making to this day. Taking their skills to levels previously unimagined many glass making and

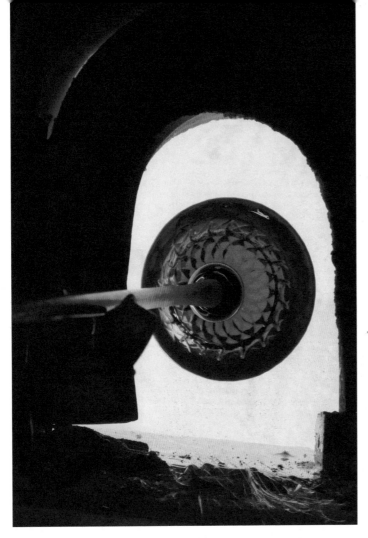

– white threads of glass running through the body of very pure colourless glass; and they also introduced ice glass, a technique that involved plunging hot molten glass into cold water causing a crackle effect. Skilled at diamond point engraving, they learned to add copper powder to the mix to create a rich green coloured glass. By the end of the seventeenth century they were producing blown sheets of mirror glass, and Venetian techniques would spread to Germany, Holland and elsewhere by the

> *Improved cylinder sheet was used to glaze the Crystal Palace – that great Victorian monument to glass*

eighteenth century. German glass makers also introduced important innovations, including glass-decorating techniques such as undercutting and faceting.

The development of lead crystal is usually attributed to an English glass maker, George Ravenscroft (1618–1681), who discovered that by using large amounts of lead oxide as a flux instead of potash he could produce a bright sparkling glass that was ideal for engraving. His glass was patented in 1674.

Crown glass continued to be used in windows into the nineteenth century, when it was replaced by various processes, including cylinder glass, first made in France and Germany in the eighteenth century and then in Britain in the mid nineteenth. It was created by blowing and manipulating a molten ball of glass to form a large, even, hollow cylinder (larger than for broad sheet, therefore making much bigger panes) which was

ABOVE *A glass vase is turned in a Kiln on the island of Murano, Italy. Traditional glass making became established there in the thirteenth century, and since then it has been known as 'glass island'.*

RIGHT *By the sixteenth century Venetian glass makers had developed a new type of decoration, composed of opaque-white lattimo cane which were actually embedded in the glass itself.*

decorating techniques were invented or at least refined by the Venetians. Well placed to learn from the advanced glass blowing and glass enamelling techniques developed in the Middle East, Venice had more than 3,000 glass blowers on the small island of Murano by the fifteenth century. The craftsmen in the city were at the peak of their powers over the next two centuries. By the mid fifteenth century they had developed their own clear crystal glass; in the sixteenth century opaque lattimo glass and filigree

RIGHT *The lines and distortions of old glass occurred when the molten glass was pulled and stretched over the cames. Because only small, flat sheets of glass could be made at this time, these windows had lots of smaller panels.*

then cooled, cut open and reheated so that it could be flattened. Improved cylinder sheet was used to glaze the Crystal Palace – that great Victorian monument to glass.

In 1848 there was a new industrial invention, cast plate glass: the molten glass was removed from the furnace in big iron ladles, from which it was thrown against a cast iron rolling table and rolled into sheets by an iron roller (which could be smooth or patterned). The sheets were trimmed while still warm and soft and then cooled slowly in an annealing tunnel.

In the early twentieth century machine-made glass started to replace hand-blown flat glass on a large scale. Drawn sheet glass was created by dipping a 'leader' into molten glass in a vat and drawing it up continuously so that a growing film or ribbon of glass hardened just above the vat as it cooled. Today 90 per cent of flat glass in the world is float glass, invented by Sir Alastair Pilkington as recently as the 1950s. Molten glass is poured into a bath of molten tin, on which the glass levels out as it floats on the tin, cooling slowly and leaving the bath in a continuous smooth ribbon before passing into the annealing tunnel.

GLASS IN BRITAIN

Ancient glass can survive almost indefinitely even if buried deep beneath the ground. The biggest risk, of course, is accidental breakage, though modern conservators are extraordinarily good at piecing glass artefacts back together even when they are dealing with thousands of fragments. Most early glass in Britain is held in museums or,

RIGHT *The Portland vase, like the majority of cameo-glass vessels, was made by the dip-overlay method, whereby an elongated bubble of glass was partially dipped into a crucible of white glass, before the two were blown together.*

BELOW *The glass fish bottle, from el-Amarna, Egypt, was made by trailing molten glass over a core of clay mixture. Coloured glass rods were then wrapped around it and dragged to create a fish-scale pattern.*

in the case of medieval glass, fixed in church windows, but so much glass was being made by, say, the late seventeenth century that much from this period at least survives in private hands.

The British Museum in London holds some wonderful examples of early glass from many parts of the world, including a spectacular blue glass jug inscribed for Thutmose III and made in an Egyptian workshop around 1400BCE. There is a stunning glass bottle in the form of a fish (tilapia) from ancient Egypt, dated to

> *So much glass was being made by the late seventeenth century that much from this period at least survives in private hands*

the eighteenth dynasty (1390–1336BCE). Glass vessels seem to have been primarily functional rather than ritual objects with their main use as containers for cosmetics or precious oils. There is also a fluted bottle made around 1300BCE from Ur in what is now known as southern Iraq. It was made during the Kassite Dynasty using dark brown glass decorated with thin delicate threaded lines of blue glass. While it was still hot the glass had also been decorated with chevrons and fluted.

Other very early examples in the Museum include a Greek bowl, made around 200BCE, using a complex double-layer technique. The bowl shows a floral design in gold leaf that has been fixed between two layers of clear glass – effectively between two glass bowls, one fitted neatly and precisely into the other. The first bowl was probably made using molten glass pressed over a mould. The decoration was then added to this bowl before the second glass bowl was fitted, and

the whole thing would then have been heated until the two glass bowls fused together.

Another item in the collection is a very rare and beautiful pillar-moulded bowl that has survived from the first century CE. Made in Italy using naturally coloured blue glass, this bowl would have been an expensive item. Even more spectacular is a facet-cut Roman glass dish showing Bellerophon and a winged horse which was made in the fourthth century.

But perhaps the rarest and most beautiful ancient glass artefact in the British Museum is the Portland Vase. This Roman vase is made in what is known as cameo glass and, worldwide, only around a dozen similar examples are known. Experts believe Roman cameo glass was made during a period that lasted only for one or at most two generations between the first and second centuries CE. Given its beauty and the complex and difficult process used to make it, cameo glass was clearly made exclusively for the Roman elite. The Portland Vase – named after the Dukes of Portland who once owned it – was made using two layers of glass: a rich, dark blue under layer with

LEFT *This glass bottle was discovered in a grave at Ur, Southen Iraq, dating to the Kassite period, approximately 1531 to 1155BCE. It was made from dark brown glass moulded on a core and decorated with a turquoise thread wound around the vessel. The hot glass was then combed to create a chevron pattern and fluted body.*

RIGHT *The 'blobbing' effect on this Roman glass jug, which dates from 40–75CE, was achieved by rolling soft glass on a blowpipe over scattered chips of coloured glass, which became embedded and fused to the surface. After reheating, the vessel would be blown and finished.*

FAR RIGHT *The 28 stained glass windows at St Mary's Church, Gloucestershire, are the most complete set from the medieval period in Britain. They were installed c.1500–15CE and illustrate bible stories from the New and Old Testament. This panel is the Last Judgement.*

a layer of pure white glass on top. Once the vase was complete, the white glass was carefully cut away in the shape of figures and animals leaving it starkly outlined against the blue glass background.

One of the greatest recent glass finds in Britain occurred in 2009 when an extremely rare first or second century millefiori (thousand flowers) dish was unearthed during a dig near London's Aldgate. The dish, which can be seen at the Museum of London, was carefully made from hundreds of tiny glass petals fused together in a repeating pattern.

Roman glass survives in relatively large quantities mainly because so much of it was made. Museums across the world have examples of Roman jugs, bowls and square mould-blown bottles, as well as oil lamps and other artefacts. Most of this everyday glassware was made at a few major centres in Eastern Europe.

By the early Christian era glass manufacture had come a long way from its ancient origins, but glass items would still have been beyond the reach of all but the rich. A fine example of post-Roman glass, again held by the British Museum, is a sixth century Sutri drinking horn, which was found in Italy. Decorated with delicate latticework, the horn is of blue glass with white decoration and loosely imitates an ox horn. The Museum also has a particularly rich collection of very early glass pendants, including a number of beautiful gold glass ones made between the third and sixth

century, as well gold glass tiles from sixth and seventh century Syria.

Remarkably well-preserved Germanic glass found in Anglo-Saxon graves, particularly in the East of England and made between 400 and 700CE, includes cone-shaped

{ *Roman glass survives in relatively large quantities mainly because so much of it was made* }

beakers and drinking horns, some twisted to create a distinctive decorative pattern. Other Germanic beakers from this period are decorated with what look like numerous regularly spaced claws.

The Victoria and Albert Museum's superb collection of early glass concentrates on the gradual development of different glass-making techniques and styles of decoration. It also has a collection of modern art glass, including examples of cast glass. The best collection of English glass is held at the Broadfield House Glass Museum at Stourbridge in Gloucestershire, where glass has been made for more than four hundred years.

But arguably the greatest quantity of surviving early glass in Britain lies not in our museums but in our churches – across Britain, fragments and sometimes whole windows of medieval stained glass can be seen, often in out of the way and little known churches. The complete cycle of stained glass windows at St Mary's, Fairford,

ABOVE *The Adam Delving window at Canterbury Cathedral, Kent is some of the earliest surviving stained glass in Europe.*
RIGHT *The famous rose window at York Minster.*

made as early as 1500CE. Less well known is the 23m (76ft) tall Great East Window, also at York Minster, made perhaps a century earlier by John Thornton. This is the largest single surviving example of medieval stained glass in the world.

Like York, Canterbury Cathedral has a number of fine examples of very early stained glass but particularly the window showing Adam delving. This remarkable window dates to 1176.

> *Glasses, jugs, bowls and bottles were all being made in large quantities by the eighteenth century*

Glasses, jugs, bowls and bottles were all being made in large quantities by the eighteenth century but industrialisation in the nineteenth century expanded manufacture even further. By the end of the nineteenth century a reaction had set in, and the movement spearheaded by William Morris saw a return to hand-made glass but particularly stained glass. William Morris's company made glass using designs by some of the great painters of the day, in particular Edward Burne-Jones and Dante Gabriel Rossetti. The Victoria and Albert Museum has some fine examples made between 1862 and 1890 and it also displays modern 'art glass' by such masters as Bernard Dejonghe, Danny Perkins and Toots Zynsky.

in Gloucestershire is a good example. This small church has some of the best surviving late medieval glass in Britain. Twenty-eight windows have survived almost intact showing bible stories, the prophets, apostles and saints. The windows were made shortly after 1500 and probably by the king's glazier Bernard Flower.

The tradition of creating rose windows in churches – originally a French gothic invention – reached its height in Britain in the spectacular example at York Minster. Like the Fairford glass this remarkable window was

In the modern world glass has been developed for a remarkable number of applications. The new roof of the Great Court at the British Museum, for example, is an extraordinary mosaic of huge sheets of glass that allow the maximum amount

of light to fall on the vast space below. The roof covers two acres and uses more than 3,300 pieces of glass, no two of which are the same shape.

Of course there is nothing new about using glass as a roofing material. Perhaps even more spectacular than the Great Court roof are the railway station roofs at Kings Cross and Paddington. Other magnificent examples can be found in the huge Victorian glasshouses at Kew Gardens and in the now vanished Crystal Palace, built in Hyde Park in London for the Great Exhibition of 1851. This splendid monument to glass, devised by Joseph Paxton, used 900,000 square feet of glass but only remained in Hyde Park for six months; it was then relocated to Penge and was finally destroyed by fire in 1936. What a vision that conjures up of a mountain of molten glass!

ABOVE *The Great Court at The British Museum has a grand glass and steel roof. The canopy was constructed from 3,312 panes of glass, no two of which are alike.*

LEFT *The most striking feature of London's Paddington station is the glazed domed roof over the main train shed, designed by Isambard Kingdom Brunel.*

METALWORKING

The Craft of Metalworking

The traditional blacksmith's forge immediately conveys the nature of working with iron: fierce heat, glowing red-hot metal, sparks flying, the ringing sound of the hammer beating iron on iron, perhaps a horse being shod in the yard, or the hiss of steam as the smith's hot iron tyre is tightened to its wooden wheel by being plunged into cold water by the neighbouring wheelwright. But many metals other than iron can be crafted by hand.

Today we know of around eighty-six different metals, but before 1800 only twenty-four metals were known, and before 1700 that figure drops to twelve. During Antiquity – a period that includes the Greek, Roman and Egyptian worlds – just seven metals were known: gold, silver, tin, lead, iron, mercury and copper. All were highly valued, but gold above all.

Gold, famously, can sometimes be 'panned' as pure small nuggets, flakes and grains by sifting through alluvial material in stream beds, if you know where to look. But it is only rarely that other metals can be found in this 'native' state: most are locked away in their rock ores and you need to know not only where to look for the ores but also how to extract the pure metal from them. The ores often contain a mixture of metals, which have to be teased apart by various processes. For example, most silver production today is from silver-bearing ores of metals like lead, copper, zinc, tin and gold.

Tin is found in cassiterite, which is associated with granite formations – hence historically Britain's most important tin-producing county was Cornwall, where the underlying rock is largely granite. Other major metal mining areas in Britain were historically the Lake District, the northern Pennines, Yorkshire Dales, Isle of Man, Derbyshire, West Shropshire, the Mendips and central and northern Wales. In Scotland there were some historically important silver mines; lead mines profilerated and copper was also mined. There were a couple of minor Scottish gold rushes in

> *Ores often contain a mixture of metals, which have to be teased apart by various processes*

the mid nineteenth century; and massive iron deposits were found in the Hebrides.

Iron, in fact, is found almost everywhere – around 35 per cent of the Earth's total weight is attributable to iron – but it does not generally lie around in handy pieces on or near the surface. It usually has to be extracted from various iron ores, unless you are fortunate enough to come across lumps of meteoric iron (meteorites containing a nickel/iron alloy).

EXTRACTING THE METAL

It was the discovery that metals could be extracted from seams and deposits in rocks that led to the first major developments in

ABOVE *Banded iron formations are a distinctive type of rock consisting of repeated thin layers of iron oxides, shown here on the sedimentary rock found in the Sottish highlands.*

LEFT *The cast alloy of copper and tin is bronze, which has been useful to man since earliest times. Excavations at Parys Mountain copper mine in North Wales have revealed sub-surface debris which is nearly 4,000 years old.*

metalworking. The original discovery may well have been made by chance: people noticed that rocks on which they had built their cooking fires sometimes left small deposits of metal, melted from the ore by the heat.

Deliberately extracting metals from their ores was first carried out by heating metal-bearing rocks. If the rocks were on the surface a fire could simply be built against them and, if the particular metal had a low enough melting point, molten metal would ooze out.

But metal-bearing rocks were often embedded or underground, and so needed to be mined. Until explosives began to be used in mining after the seventeenth century this meant hacking at the rocks by hand with picks, hammers and wedges to split them. In underground mines the chunks were then loaded into baskets, dragged on sledges and winched up a shaft to the surface. If the underground rock proved too hard to split manually, a fire was built against the rock face and left overnight; in the morning water was splashed against the hot rock, causing it to shatter.

After mining, the next step is to separate metals and their compounds from the raw ore and this is the essence of smelting. In technical terms, smelting is the fusion of an ore, with suitable fluxes to produce a melt consisting of two layers: a top slag of flux and gangue (valueless) minerals, with the molten pure metal below.

Many ores produce metal compounds which need to be chemically 'reduced' to liberate the pure metal. Sulphide ores, for example, can be reduced by heating the ore in the presence of oxygen, so the sulphur is oxidised to sulphur dioxide, leaving pure metal. Reduction traditionally relied on coke and charcoal to produce carbon as the reducing agent. The oldest method was

simply to build a large fire out in the open, pile up big pieces of metal-rich ore on it and rely on two days of strong winds to fan the bonfire. The next major development was enclosed smelting mills in which foot-pumped or water-powered bellows took the place of unreliable natural wind forces to roar up the flames: first the ore was broken or crushed with a hammer, then it was placed in a wood-burning furnace and finally transferred for re-melting in a charcoal-fired second furnace.

The next development was cupola smelting, invented in the eighteenth century, in which the fuel and the ore were kept separate; the slag was raked off and the molten metal (e.g. lead) flowed into iron pots and then ladled into moulds to produce ingots, or pigs, of the pure metal.

A more modern method is electrolytic reduction, whereby a strong electric current is passed through the molten metal compound. The latest technique is to use microbes to extract metals from their ores.

The end result, whether several thousand years ago or today, was that the metalworker acquired the raw material of his craft – a metal – in a relatively pure state. Dealers sold their mined and purified gold and silver to craftsmen as bars or gold leaf; ironmakers offered their finished iron and steel for sale as bars, rods and billets ready to be worked by blacksmiths and others. Other metal dealers offered, for example, the raw material used by tinsmiths in the form of ready-made sheets of iron, coated with a layer of tin. Metal dealers also sold readymade pewter in sheets and billets for craftsmen to cast and carve.

TYPES OF METAL AND THEIR USES

Metals can be broadly divided between base and precious metals. The latter include gold, silver, platinum and the like. The base metals are sometimes subdivided into ferrous and non-ferrous. Ferrous metals (all of which are magnetic) are those that contain iron. Non-ferrous metals don't have iron in them and are not magnetic; they include, for example, copper, aluminium, zinc, nickel, tin and lead.

ABOVE *Native silver is the purest kind, found in igneous and sedimentary ore like galena. It is formed in veins of rock that have hot water flowing through and around them.*

LEFT *Approximately 10,000 lead industry sites survive in England. They span from the later Bronze Age until the present day, such as the lead smelting mill at Hard Level Gill, North Yorkshire.*

{ *Dealers sold their mined and purified gold and silver to craftsmen in bars or as gold leaf* }

Alloys are mixtures of two or more elements, the major component being metal. Combining metals in this way creates a material that is harder, less brittle and less liable to corrosion. The best known alloys are bronze (an alloy of copper and tin) and those of iron combined with carbon: cast iron, wrought iron and steel.

Hypoallergenic alloys such as nickel and titanium are used to make items such as artificial hips to space age metals used to make moon landing craft – metal encompasses the whole range of human activity in the modern world.

Gold is used in everything from jewellery and dental fillings to cooking and semi-conductors; nickel is used in microchips; coltan in mobile phones; and neodymium, lanthanum and dysprosium in hybrid (electric and petrol) vehicles.

The more unusual uses to which metals have been put – and today these include

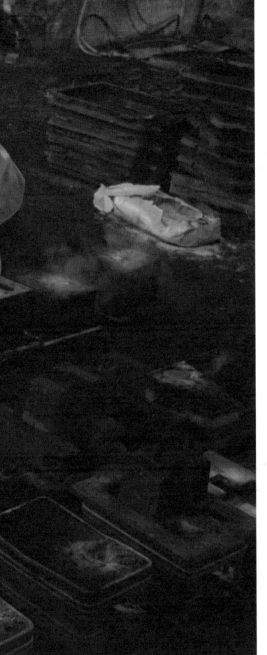

conditioners – all of these rely on the ability of humans to manipulate metals in countless different ways.

But modern factory techniques have come to be possible only because for centuries craftsmen slowly learned of the extraordinary uses to which metal could be put.

METALWORKING TECHNIQUES

Once a metal has been mined and extracted in its pure form ready for transformation by metalworkers, there are three stages that are broadly common to all types of metalworking. The first is 'forming', or deforming the metal, using heat, pressure or mechanical force; forming processes include casting molten metal, forging, rolling and extrusion. The second stage is cutting – machining, drilling, grinding, filing, burning, milling, turning and so on. The final stage is joining, perhaps by welding, brazing or soldering (methods using a filler metal). There may also be special processes like plating or annealing and tempering (controlled heating and cooling process that alter the properties of the metal).

LEFT Cast iron is made by remelting pig iron, often also adding quantities of scrap iron and steel. Iron is sometimes melted in a cupola blast furnace, but it is usually melted in electric induction furnaces. The molten metal is then transferred to a ladle and poured into moulds.

BELOW Several modern methods of electric welding supersede the older, traditional methods of fire welding.

{ *For centuries craftsmen slowly learned of the extraordinary uses to which metal could be put* }

metals such as lithium used in medicine – give a real sense of the extraordinary range of possibilities but they are nothing compared with the range of uses for ordinary metals that we may take for granted. Skyscrapers and road and rail bridges would be impossible to build without steel girders; railways rely heavily on steel, as does the car industry. Ships, cranes, buses, military vehicles, aircraft, clocks and watches, pipelines, oil rigs, computers, telephones, air

The shape of the anvil evolved over many centuries to provide the most useful tool for blacksmiths. The two simple holes allow for punching or clamps to be inserted, and the 'step' and 'horn' offer surfaces for creating complex shapes.

Blacksmiths

The derivation of the word 'blacksmith' has nothing to do with the tendency of metalworkers to become covered in grime during the course of their work. Blacksmiths work with black metal – iron (described as black because of its finish: the layer of fire-scale oxides or impurities left on the surface of iron when it has been heated) – and they work the metal by hitting it: 'smith' probably derives from 'smite'.

In essence the blacksmith's work involves heating iron until it is soft enough to be shaped with various hand tools. Carefully controlled heat is crucial to the art of the blacksmith and the core of any smithy is the forge: a chimney and a rectangular hearth built against one wall of the workshop for an enclosed fire that can be made extremely hot using bellows (often operated by machine these days rather than an apprentice). The fire may be fuelled with charcoal, sulphur-free coal, coke or gas.

The metal is heated until the smith recognises by its changing colour that it is ready to be worked. Heat-treated iron first becomes red, then orange and then yellow. When it becomes white it melts. For most processes the blacksmith wants the metal to reach forging heat, which is yellow-orange.

The essential equipment includes an anvil and a sledge hammer. A range of different anvils are available today but the traditional model, a heavy wrought iron or steel block weighing as much as three hundred pounds, is curved and pointed at one end, flattened and squared off at the other. The curved end is known as the horn or bick, the square end is the heel or hanging end. Near the heel are two holes: a square-shaped 'hardy' hole (into which a type of chisel known as a hardy, is set with the blade facing upwards so that the workpiece can be hammered down on to it) and a round or punching hole. Centuries of practical use produced the traditional design – a shape that allows the maximum number of jobs to be carried out quickly and easily. Despite the apparent simplicity of the anvil, highly complex pieces can be made using it.

Once the metal has been heated in the fire it is shaped on the anvil and then cooled in a trough of water kept close to hand. A sledge hammer is vital for heavy work and, when the traditional blacksmith needed a heavy blow to shape the metal, he would first use a much smaller hammer to tap on the piece being worked. This told the apprentice where to strike with the sledge hammer. In the modern blacksmith's forge a power-operated trip hammer may be used instead.

The more delicate and skilled parts of the traditional blacksmith's work require

> *Heat-treated iron first becomes red, then orange and then yellow. When it becomes white it melts*

BELOW *The correct temperature for each stage of work is judged by eye, the change in colour of the hot metal giving the smith the information he needs.*

RIGHT *The forge was once the heart of every village, supplying vital items to the community.*
BELOW *At near-welding heat a 'punch' is driven through on the anvil face and completed over the pritchel hole. Punching is preferred to drilling holes as it retains the strength of the metal.*

a range of smaller tools for measuring, handling, shaping and cutting the metal. These include creasing and leaf hammers, flatters (to remove hammer marks), all sorts of hot and cold chisels and sets, fullers, assorted punches, drifts (tapered to enlarge and smooth punched holes), mandrels (hollow cast-iron cones for forming rings, collars and hoops), bolsters (to shape the shoulders of harrow tines), tongs of different sizes to move the metal around, callipers for measuring, set-squares for testing right angles – and a good solid workbench with vices, wrenches and tool racks. Heavy-duty wire brushes are kept for removing slag from hot metal (absolutely vital to keep the piece clean) and all around are iron bars and rods hanging from the walls waiting for the blacksmith to select and transform them into something remarkable.

> *Forging involves a number of fairly straightforward working methods using a simple hammer and anvil*

Much decorative work is done in the blacksmith's forge using a swage block, which is a cast-iron block with half-rounds and V-notches cut into its edges and different-shaped holes of various sizes through its face. Swaging is a process of moulding or cutting iron into various shapes using a die. Another method of shaping is on a lathe, similar in principle to turning wood on a lathe.

Forging is the oldest blacksmithing technique. It involves a number of fairly straightforward working methods, each using a simple hammer and anvil, the skill of the smith making so much possible with these few tools.

First comes drawing down, which is a process of increasing the width or length of a piece of metal and reducing its cross-section. Drawing down can be speeded up using a fuller – a tool similar to a round-nosed chisel that hammers indentations into the metal. These indentations and their corresponding ridges are then hammered flat to draw out the length of the metal.

Bending, as the name suggests, is a simple process of heating metal and then hammering it into a bend over the anvil.

Shrinking bends metal so that it thickens on the inside of a curve. This thicker area is then hammered out over the whole length of the object being forged, so that it is slightly thicker than it was before, and is also slightly shorter because the length has been reduced in order to add thickness. Another method employed by the blacksmith is known as 'upsetting', where he is simply making the metal thicker in one place by shortening its length. The metal may be heated at one end and then hammered on that end.

Punching, as this technique is known, is used for decorating iron or for making simple holes through the metal.

Traditional forge welding involves heating two pieces of metal to be joined, ensuring they are as clean as possible (using sand or borax) and then hammering the pieces together, ensuring that the weld starts at the centre of the join and spreads slowly outwards. A skilled blacksmith may return the weld to the fire several times to ensure the best and strongest possible join. Modern oxyacetylene welding techniques make use of blow torches that can concentrate intense heat into a precise area.

The blacksmith's final job is finishing the piece. This may mean cleaning with a wire brush, a file, grinding stones or any other abrasive material.

Other metalworkers

Gold and silversmiths have traditionally made exclusive pieces for the wealthy, and this has been the case from the earliest times. Gold is so malleable that it can be moulded, twisted, stamped and decorated using far less force than required by other metals. Fine gold, at 24 carats, is so soft that decoration tends to wear away quickly. Today gold is often mixed with other metals, particularly platinum alloys, to create a harder, more durable metal. Casting gold traditionally used the lost wax method, which allows anything modelled in wax to be recreated fully and faithfully into various metals, and for a complex piece the various

gold parts would be cast (or stamped or moulded) and then soldered together. Goldsmiths obtain their raw materials either by melting old gold or buying small amounts of newly mined and refined gold from rare-metal dealers. Gold leaf is used to give ordinary materials – wooden picture frames for example – the lustre of gold but without the cost of using solid gold.

At the other end of the economic scale, tinsmiths made and repaired plates, pans cups and bowls for the poor. They were also known as tinners or whitesmiths. Using tin-plate – iron covered with tin to prevent rusting – they made and decorated practical household items. The tinsmith would buy his raw material in flat plates (hence tin-plate) of various sizes; and using few tools – a small anvil, shears, tin snips, a soldering iron, hammers and some punches – he could make and repair everything from coffee pots to plates, dishes, cups and whistles. Unlike the blacksmith, who needed a forge and lots of heavy equipment, the tinsmith travelled light, with his tools and tin in a pack on his back, which is where the idea of the tinker – the travelling tinsmith – came in. Without the tinker, people in remote districts would have had great difficulty getting their pots and pans and other metalwork repaired without a long and difficult trip to the nearest town which, for many, was almost impossible in the days before affordable transport.

Coppersmiths – or redsmiths as they are sometimes known – have traditionally made pots and kettles, fenders and trays, plates, picture frames and other smaller household objects. Copper is soft enough to shape without heating and by using simple hammers (hence copper beating), but in order to prevent the metal becoming too hard and eventually cracking it is annealed – heated and then rapidly cooled.

Locksmiths have an almost entirely

LEFT *Modern gilding is applied to many diverse surfaces by various processes, such as chemical gilding and mechanical gilding. It is used for framemaking, general woodworking, cabinet-work, decorative painting, bookbinding, and the decoration of pottery, porcelain and glass.*

separate set of skills and traditions from blacksmithing. The intricate wards and tumblers, keys and lock cases created by locksmiths are all traditionally made using files of many different shapes and sizes.

Coins have been created by hammering or stamping since the earliest times and, though modern coin-making is a sophisticated hi-tech business, the basic idea that a machine creates an impression on a small disc of metal remains unchanged.

> *Without the tinker, people in remote districts would have had great difficulty getting their pots and pans and other metalwork repaired*

Sculptors use various moulds to cast their work. At its simplest this would involve sand casting: an impression made in sand that would then be filled with molten metal. The lost wax method of casting metal involves carefully creating a wax version of the object and encasing it in clay. The clay is then fired until the wax melts and is 'lost', leaving the clay mould ready to be filled with metal to create the final cast object. The technique requires considerable skill, but almost nothing beyond the mould in the way of tools.

The blacksmith's forge is fuelled by charcoal or coke and the temperature controlled by venting it with air through a blower or bellows. Iron undergoes colour changes as it is heated, and recognising and controlling the temperature of the metal is a key skill.

The Mastercrafter

DON BARKER *is a medal holder and Fellow of the Worshipful Company of Blacksmiths and is very proud to be the first working smith to become Prime Warden of the Company for 200 years. His forty year love affair with blacksmithing has never waned and he continues to work in the forge shaping metal into beautiful things.*

Don Barker is a blacksmith with a passion for his work. He believes that metalworking is in his blood, which is hardly surprising given his ancestry.

'My male ancestors seem to have mostly been blacksmiths going right back to about 1700,' he explains, and I really believe that I've been drawn towards the work because it's as if it's there in my genes.'

But Don's route to metalwork wasn't a straightforward one, as he explains.

'My most recent blacksmithing ancestor was my grandfather and back in the 1930s when he saw what was happening in the Depression he decided that his sons should be teachers rather than blacksmiths.'

When it was Don's turn he trained as an engineer. He enjoyed the work but hated what he saw as the endless bureaucracy.

'I started to do a bit of blacksmithing in my spare time; I had a knack for it and I was enthusiastic, so a few jobs started coming in.'

He enjoyed watching the blacksmiths he worked alongside.

'I'd seen blacksmiths forging metal where I worked and was inspired by them, so I started doing it as a hobby. It took up more and more of my time and I really enjoyed it, so in 1983 when I was thirty-eight I decided to quit my job and be a full-time blacksmith. I set up a limited company and I've never looked back.'

> I started blacksmithing in my spare time, but I had a knack for it and I was enthusiastic

Don's experience as an engineer stood him in good stead when he started work as a blacksmith, but he is the first to admit that despite his enthusiasm and the spare time he had put into his passion, he still had a lot to learn.

'I did need to train and I did it through CoSIRA (Council for Small Industries in Rural Areas), a government quango that ran workshops up and down the country. I met Joe Hansom, who worked for CoSIRA, and he taught me a lot. I remember going on a CoSIRA course with Joe at Harrogate showground, which isn't that far from my home in York. In fact I did several one-week courses. Joe taught me the intricacies of forge work and how to use a power hammer to best effect.'

By this time the years of hobby blacksmithing were paying off and commissions were already coming in steadily. Don was being asked to make everything from gates and railings to pokers and firedogs.

'I thought I was doing pretty well, but it helped enormously to learn how to do intricate forging work such as making an animal head on the end of a bar of metal. That's much more difficult than it might sound, because you are working with white-hot metal and you have to shape it with a limited number of tools – just chisels and hammers.'

ABOVE *By drawing the metal out of the fire the blacksmith can gauge its temperature by looking at the colour which changes as it heats up.*

RIGHT *By holding the metal at the correct angle on the anvil, the hammer and anvil are made to work together to squeeze the metal into the required shapes.*

Like most blacksmiths, Don buys his metal in the form of bars. Stock bars of mild steel come from a stockholder. They are the basic raw material for most of Don's work.

'We buy them in a range of sizes – maybe half an inch square or an inch square or more – and we forge whatever people want. If they want decorative gates, we'll make them; if they want special railings, we'll make those too. If it can be made in metal, then we will make it.'

Part of the skill of blacksmith work is judging the correct temperature of metal for specific types of work.

'When you are heating at a forge, the general rule is the hotter the metal the softer

ABOVE *A bar along the side edge of the forge is used to hang all the various tongs the blacksmith needs to hold pieces of hot metal.*

and easier it is to work. For fire welding – that is, welding two pieces of metal together – you want it almost melting. For steel tools, which have to be very hard, you'd only heat a bar till it is red, so not nearly as hot.'

Once Don has judged the temperature, he gets down to the business of shaping and cutting.

'The real skill is in forging – doing scroll work for gates, for example, or making what we call fishtail end scrolls, bolt-end scrolls, leaf work or ha'penny snub scrolls.

'All this decorative work takes a lot of practise and skill. You just can't learn to do it overnight. For most of our work wherever possible we don't use tongs to hold the bar – we just make sure the bar is long enough to hold at one end while working on the other end. If it's a short bar though we will use specially-fitting tongs.'

Watching a blacksmith at work is a remarkably satisfying experience. With a minimum of fuss and seemingly effortlessly he can turn a plain bar of metal into something complex and decorative.

'Apart from getting the forging temperature right, there's an art in striking the metal in just the right way. And it's this creative skill that I believe I've inherited from my blacksmith ancestors.'

> *When heating at a forge, the general rule is the hotter the metal the softer and easier it is to work*

ABOVE **Management of the fire is critical. The blacksmith must be careful not to leave the metal in the fire or it will burn and ruin.**

BELOW **In addition to the anvil, the blacksmith's tools include hammers, tongs, scrolling irons, chisels, horns and hardies.**

Light taps with the hammer produce the delicate work, but Don is always happy to use the power hammer to take the backbreaking element out of heavier work.

'We don't use the power hammer for delicate work like leaf scrolls but it is very useful for more straightforward work on heavier pieces of metal.'

According to Don, experience is a key factor. Skill comes with developing a sure touch and that can only happen over time.

'Each time you make a leaf scroll, or a ram's head, you get better at it and you begin to put your own stamp on things. Blacksmiths always recognise their own and other people's work. There is standard practice in forging but beyond that you are free to add as much of yourself as you like.'

His meticulous description of making a complex item for the top of a poker reveals something of the skill involved.

'You start by forging what we call a flat piece, which you split. Each side is then bent back, fire welded and textured with chisels to make the face, the ram's nostrils and what-have-you. Then we use tongs to twist the horns. A ram's head made like that sounds pretty straightforward but it only becomes so after years of practice. I reckon it would take me about twenty minutes to make one and, although I've made many, I never lose the sense of satisfaction in making one really well.'

In addition to many local commissions for gates and railings, curtain rails and even

shackles, Don has worked on some major blacksmithing projects.

'I did a really important job for the front of Westminster Abbey – a set of traditional gas lamps. I also made four six feet high bronze lamps and sixty five metres of bronze handrailing for the Queen Mother's memorial in the Mall. Closer to home, we made a pair of stainless steel gates for a park in York after winning a design competition. Those lamps for the Queen Mother's memorial had a lot of work in them – they took eight months to make, so you can see it's slow careful work. But for all our work, however large or small, it's not about speed, the important thing is to get it right.'

ABOVE **Don is never happier than when he is in the forge surrounded by all his traditional tools and heaps of metal – and a roaring fire.**

The blacksmith uses hammers and punches to cut and bend bars or strips of metal heated in the forge. Working with the flat strips by punching in designs is known as repoussé

The Tradition of Metalworking

It took much longer for metals to be discovered and methods of processing them to be developed than for plant resources. The tradition of metalworking stretches back perhaps 10,000 years, when gold was already being fashioned into jewellery. Copper has been worked for some nine millennia and the alloy, bronze, for perhaps 5,000 years; iron was being worked a thousand years later. The techniques have evolved over the centuries but the essentials are still practised by craft workers today.

The earliest surviving metalwork comes down to us in the form of jewellery. Copper and gold jewellery, crafted by the Sumerians in the Middle East from about 7000BCE can be seen today in several collections including at the British Museum.

The ancient Egyptians developed metalworking to levels unthinkable in earlier epochs – some would argue that their goldsmiths' work has never been surpassed. The burial mask of Tutankhamen is perhaps the best known example of goldsmiths' work in the world, but this lavish, intricate mask would have been created in a workshop that no doubt made far more impressive gold masks for other, more important pharaohs. Images of gods and goddesses, tutelary spirits, priests, noblemen, pharaohs, cats, scarab beetles, crocodiles and sacred bulls were made in cast bronze in enormous numbers over the thousands of years the pharaohs ruled.

In China, Japan and Korea, bronze casting was understood from at least 3000BCE. Many examples of bronze bowls have survived from this early period, particularly the Chinese ding, a cauldron that stood on three legs and was probably used for cooking.

Apart from these domestic items the bulk of early surviving bronzes from Asia are religious: huge numbers of bronze statues of the numerous Hindu gods exist, as well as ancient bronze and gilt statues associated with the Buddha. These remain, in their thousands, in the temples and shrines for which they were made, but fine examples can also be seen in many British museums.

In India, very early metalwork survives in a number of places but there are few more remarkable examples than the Iron Pillar of Delhi. The pillar is fascinating not just because it has survived since it was made sometime between 375 and 414CE but also because it has not corroded: studies have

shown that the high-temperature method by which is was made ensured that a layer of highly protective particles remained on the surface of the metal. Almost seven metres (23ft) tall, the pillar is 98 per cent wrought iron and weighs more than six tonnes. It stands in the ruins of a Jain (a Hindu sect) temple complex. The inscription on the pillar explains that it was erected in honour of Lord Vishnu, the most important of all the Hindu gods. What fascinates those interested in metalwork is that it would have taken a very advanced forging process to produce such a remarkable artefact.

In Europe very early metalwork was at least as important for weapons as for

ABOVE *The iron pillar of Delhi has not corroded due to its 'protective film', formed catalytically by phosphorous.*

LEFT *The metal for the golden coffin of Tutankhamun was beaten from heavy gold sheet, and varies in thickness. from 0.25 to 0.3 cm (0.098 to 0.118in).*

personal, religious, domestic and agricultural items. The Roman historian Polybius and Roman poet Plutarch stated that Celtic iron swords needed to be straightened after just a few blows – the Celts could forge iron but, unlike the Romans, had little idea how to make it hard enough to withstand repeated blows. Many examples of early iron swords survive, though usually heavily corroded. By the late medieval period iron swords and daggers were being made from harder iron.

{ *The salvaging of Henry VIII's flagship the* Mary Rose *revealed a number of surprising early metal artefacts* }

Meanwhile wrought-iron chainmail had been fending off attack by blades and spears and saving the lives of countless warriors since Roman times. By the Tudor period plate armour was being made and, though expensive, heavy and cumbersome, it offered a remarkably high level of protection against firearms. However, gun-making improved in tandem with these improvements in armour until, by the end of the English Civil War, armour was all but obsolete.

The salvaging of Henry VIII's flagship the *Mary Rose* revealed a number of surprising early metal artefacts, including finely made metal syringes that were apparently used to inject syphilitic sailors with warm mercury! The ship, which sank in 1545 while defending Portsmouth, was one of the most heavily armed vessels in the royal fleet: she carried 91 guns, including two cannons that fired 64lb (29kg) castiron shot. Cast iron was of major importance in the development of fire power, both for gun barrels and for shot.

Before aircraft, perhaps the most significant change in military hardware achieved through the use of metal was the iron-clad ship. First introduced in the 1850s to protect vulnerable wooden hulls from naval guns, the move signalled the beginning of the end for all timber-built military (and ultimately commercial) shipping.

METALWORK DEVELOPMENTS

The importance of the changes in metal use over the course of human history can be judged by the very words we use to describe our past: references to the Bronze Age and the Iron Age reflect momentous changes in human history that affected everyday life in ways that were profound.

Native metals, readily to hand in either a pure state or as an alloy, are rare but they could have been found by early man as nuggets on stream beds where they could simply be picked up. That is how it was with gold, which almost certainly would have been the first metal to be worked simply because it does not have to be refined in any way and is soft enough to mould and shape with minimal technology or effort.

Silver can also be found in pure nuggets, but not very often: it is usually combined with other elements, or in ores on its own or with other metals. Other metals that are very occasionally found in the native form are copper, tin and meteoric iron, and these were used in not just antiquity but also prehistoric times.

RIGHT A Celtic sword with scabbard, from the early La Tène Period, 400/350BCE. Scabbards were generally made from two plates of iron, and suspended from a belt made of iron links.
FAR RIGHT The iron-hulled ship was a huge step forward in naval design. Brunel's SS Great Britain combined this innovation with the equally revolutionary screw propeller.

Discovery of smelting and alloys

It is possible that deliberate smelting was being practiced as far back as some 8,500 years ago, but only in very limited quantities. By far the biggest challenge was to find larger amounts of ores, and develop the techniques to extract metals from them on a scale substantial enough to make a difference to human progress. And succeeding at that took quite a while longer.

Iron was originally extracted using charcoal to obtain sufficient heat for the smelting process

Copper was one of the early metals to be exploited and many archaeologists talk about a 'Copper Age' preceding the Bronze Age. Like gold, copper would have been too soft to be used for much beyond personal adornment, though copper axes more than 5,000 years old have been found, and it is thought copper was being used for tools some 9,000 years ago. In North America nuggets and veins of pure copper were being exploited from gravels around Lake Superior 6,000 years ago and made into weapons and decorative objects.

In some parts of the world, such as the Near East, Asia and Greece, it had been discovered by 3000BCE that the addition of tin to molten copper produced the much harder but still malleable alloy, bronze. The Bronze Age had begun, though it only came to Britain (an important source of both copper and tin) about a thousand years later (2500–700BCE).

Bronze transformed life for humans across Europe, the Middle East and beyond because it could be made into relatively hard implements including swords and tools, pots and bowls. The problem with bronze was that the raw materials needed to make it were available only in certain locations, so it was expensive to obtain and distribute. Gold, copper and, later, bronze were so important and valuable that they were in fact used as currency. Another problem was that bronze weapon blades couldn't be sharpened: they had to be re-forged and

BELOW *A large haul of Bronze Age artefacts were uncovered in Norfolk in 2005. The 145 items, dating from about 800BCE, included axe heads, spear heads, sword parts, tools and ingots.*

weapons of the period were constantly recycled for this reason.

The Iron Age dawns

Iron has a higher melting point than copper, tin and bronze, hence greater heat was needed for smelting it. But the ore is much more common and so when a method was discovered for melting and purifying it, harder and more durable tools and weapons quickly became available across a much wider geographical and social spectrum than had been the case with bronze.

In some parts of the world they were already smelting iron to make implements some 4,000 years ago, in parallel with bronze. But the 'Iron Age' is classically defined as beginning some 3,000 years ago in some of the ancient civilisations and much later elsewhere: Britain's Iron Age is usually defined as the period from 700BCE until the Roman Conquest in 43CE.

Steel was also used from the early days, as well as iron: steelwork some 4,000 years old has been found in Turkey, for example. Steel is an alloy of iron and carbon, often with the addition of other elements such as nickel, chromium and vanadium

Iron was originally extracted using charcoal to obtain sufficient heat for the smelting process. In England – the centre of iron production for more than a thousand years – from the end of the Roman period until well into the Tudor era, was the well-wooded Weald of Kent and Sussex. Here clay furnaces were used to smelt relatively small but significant amounts of iron. The introduction of blast furnaces from France in the late fifteenth century changed everything, because instead of producing a few pounds of iron each day a furnace might now be able to produce as much as a ton. Ponds were dug to create waterheads to supply power for driving the massive hammers and huge bellows

needed by the ironworks.

The next big development in iron production came with James Watts' invention of a reliable steam engine in 1777. This enabled a number of processes to be dramatically improved, but especially hammering and operating the bellows that sent a blast of air (from which we get the term blast furnace) into the forge.

As the forests of Europe gradually diminished under the ceaseless demand for charcoal, Abraham Darby (1750–1791) discovered that the more widely available

ABOVE *A blast furnace is a large, steel stack lined with refractory brick. Iron ore, coke and limestone are introduced into the furnace from the high ground above, and preheated air is blown into the bottom.*

ABOVE *Torcs were made from intertwined metal strands, usually gold or bronze. The superb Snettisham gold torc is made of multiple strands, with simple loop terminals. It had been wedged into a pit, but sprang back into shape when it was removed some 2,000 years later.*

coke (derived from coal rather than wood) could be used for smelting , just as successfully as charcoal for smelting.

By now cast iron, as well as wrought iron, was being produced by re-melting the pig iron in a blast furnace. Wrought iron has a very low carbon content and contains slag, giving the alloy a fibrous grain like wood. As a result it is malleable and easily welded. Cast iron on the other hand has a higher carbon content and is a much more brittle alloy, making it no good for items with sharp edges or requiring flexibility. But it is immensely strong under compression (though not under tension) and makes a good engineering material, resisting destruction and rust.

Steel can contain varying proportions of carbon: it becomes harder and stronger as

{ *Metal lasts longer than wood, but usually has a far shorter life than stone* }

the carbon content increases but less ductile. Steel can also include other metals such as chromium, nickel and vanadium. The effects of the mass production of good quality cheap steel in the seventeenth century changed the world profoundly, with an almost endless list of uses that sum up what it means to live in the modern world.

With a lower carbon content than cast iron, the mass production of steel became possible in the 1850s when Sir Henry Bessemer (1813–1898) invented what came to be known as the Bessemer Process. He worked on the principle of blasting air through pig iron to remove impurities, reducing the carbon content to the right level.

MASTERPIECES IN METAL

Metal lasts longer than wood, but usually has a far shorter life than stone simply because in most cases (gold, silver and to some extent bronze are exceptions) it will corrode unless carefully looked after. This probably explains why very early metalwork is rare in Britain.

The main exceptions to this include Celtic and Roman coins and statues (more usually parts of statues) and gold and silver work such as the magnificent Snettisham treasure, the largest deposit of gold, silver and bronze artefacts dating from the Iron Age ever found in Britain. Held in the British Museum, the centrepiece of this group is the Great Torc, a large solid gold neck ring with a human head carved at one end. The design of numerous other Snettisham torcs, in silver, bronze and gold, suggest a Gallo-Belgic origin for much of the treasure (in other words they were imported), and the hoard, which comprises hundreds of items, including gold coins, may well be the royal treasure of Boudicca, the Queen of the Celtic Iceni tribe, who died in 60CE.

A similarly superb collection of fine early metalwork can be seen, again in the British Museum, in the Hoxne Hoard, probably the finest single find of Roman metalwork in Britain. Beautifully worked gold and silver jewellery, tableware and even silver toothpicks were found alongside a staggering 15,000 gold, silver and bronze coins. More than 550 of the coins are gold solidi, the rest silver siliquae, the main silver coin of the late Roman Empire.

But the Hoxne Hoard contains no single piece as fabulous as the Roman silver tray at the British Museum. Apart from its beauty and size – it measures 51 x 38cm (20 x 15in) – the

BELOW *The Hoxne Hoard, Suffolk, was buried for safety towards the end of the Roman era. Uncovered in 1992, 24 bronze coins, 565 gold coins, 14,191 silver coins, plus hundreds of gold and silver spoons, jewellery, and statues, were discovered.*

LEFT *One of four 'Empress' pepper pots from the Hoxne Hoard. This example takes the form of a hollow silver bust of an Imperial lady of the late-Roman period.*

RIGHT *The gilt-bronze tomb effigy of Queen Eleanor of Castile in Westminster Abbey. It was cast using the lost wax process by William Torel in 1291.*

tray is important because it is decorated with splendidly realistic hunting scenes, shepherds and musicians but also has early Christian inscriptions. It was probably made soon after the Romans finally abandoned Britain in 410ce.

Roman metalwork, including bronze statues, weapons, shield bosses and smaller personal items – particularly lamps – can be found in many British museums. Most Roman bronze statues are fragmentary but the Gosbecks Mercury, a bronze figurine of the Roman messenger god, is perhaps the finest because it is the only almost complete statue of its kind in Britain. It can be seen in Colchester Castle Museum.

> *A great deal of corroded Roman ironwork survives in the form of sword and dagger blades*

A great deal of corroded Roman ironwork survives in the form of sword and dagger blades together with far better preserved bronze weapons, ceremonial bowls and cups. The great Anglo-Saxon poem Beowulf (probably first written in the eighth century) describes how it was common in warfare for the gold fittings of swords and other weapons to be stripped by the victors. This is how the Staffordshire hoard of Anglo-Saxon gold (found in July 2009) seems to have been gathered together before being buried for safe keeping. The huge hoard, including about 1,500 items, mostly in gold, probably dates to the seventh century and the workmanship is superb.

Soon after the Norman Conquest in 1066 the rapid programme of building castles and churches across England led to an explosion in the amount and quality of metalwork being produced. Much of this would have been in the form of religious objects made in silver and gold – candlesticks, communion cups and so on. It was invariably melted down and sold during the Reformation.

However, wrought iron was also widely used at this time and a number of very early – and very fine – pieces have survived. These are mostly wrought iron grilles and gates, or strapwork (decorative bands of forged iron) on doors. Medieval churches in many parts of Britain have timber doors with fine strapwork across their timbers; and church railings, though rare survivals, occasionally reveal fine craftsmanship.

Perhaps the finest example of complex patterned grille work by a medieval

blacksmith is on the tomb of Eleanor of Castile (1244–1290) in Westminster Abbey. It is the work of Thomas of Leighton Buzzard, about whom almost nothing else is known. The tomb also has a gilt bronze effigy made in 1291 by goldsmith William Torel.

Cast iron firebacks were made from the first introduction of the chimney in the late medieval period and they survive in both private and National Trust houses. They were designed to protect the brickwork from heat but also to project the heat into the room.

From the Tudor period, the silver gilt Mostyn salt cellar, now in London's Victoria and Albert Museum, is an example of a particular and very popular type of table ornament that was designed to show off the wealth of its owner (and almost certainly not used for salt). It was made in 1586 and would have been placed on the high table at the host's side.

By the late seventeenth and early eighteenth centuries gold and silver work was being produced in large quantities to show off the status of individual families. The baroque buffet silver of the Earl of Macclesfield, also now in the Victoria and Albert Museum, is an extraordinary example of this kind of thing: beautifully and elaborately decorated, the wine cooler alone is big enough to hold fifty bottles.

Garden sculpture showing classical figures grew in popularity in the eighteenth century, and some of the best examples of cast lead statuary can be found in the work of Andrew Carpenter (1677–1737), whose statue of Greek mythological hero Meleager is on show in the Victoria and Albert Museum.

> *By the late seventeenth and early eighteenth centuries gold and silver work was being produced in large quantities*

The railings at London's St Paul's Cathedral, made in 1714, are a superb example of decorative cast iron. The Industrial Revolution dramatically increased the amount of cast iron being produced and perhaps the best example of its use can be seen in the world's first cast iron bridge – Abraham Darby's Iron Bridge in Shropshire, completed in 1781.

By the end of the eighteenth century, wrought iron balusters, gates and railings were being produced in profusion for the new country and town houses of the merchant classes. Superb examples can be seen in the Victoria and Albert Museum, but they also survive in many ordinary houses.

Spectacular ironwork can be seen in the roofs of many nineteenth century railway stations in Britain but especially Paddington and King's Cross Stations in London. In the early days of the railways, the magnificent steam locomotives were also made of cast iron.

The modern era has thrown up a mass of decorative and structural metalwork but most of it factory produced and made in mild steel, though often copying wrought iron designs of old. The tradition continues though with striking statues, such as the welded, bolted and riveted construction of Anthony Gormley's iconic Angel of the North, and the modern artist-blacksmith's are still producing fine, bespoke ironwork such as the gates to Shakespeare's Globe theatre.

RIGHT *Andrew Carpenter's cast lead figure of Meleager, made about 1720–30.*

FAR RIGHT *Members of the British Artist Blacksmiths Association created the ornamental Bankside gates of London's Globe Theatre, with Brian Russell as the lead Blacksmith.*

WEAVING

The Craft of Weaving

Weaving is the creation of a fabric by passing threads over and under
each other at right angles so that they become interlaced. Today weaving
is largely a mechanised process churning out huge quantities of fabric
at high speed, but traditional handloom weaving is still carried out by
craft workers all over Britain, creating original fabrics and articles using
equipment that has changed little over the centuries.

Fabric is essential in all our lives. From Harris Tweed jackets to silk shirts and cotton socks, we rely on woven material to keep us warm and dry, but that is only the beginning so far as woven material is concerned.

Of course clothing is the commonest use for woven materials and given the constraints of clothing the human body, which has not altered that much in thousands of years, it is perhaps not surprising that clothing materials have changed little – we still use wool and silk, cotton and linen just as our Roman and Egyptian ancestors did. Linen provided shirts at far lower cost in the time before cotton; and as recently as World War I nettles were being grown to provide hemp-like fibre for prisoner-of-war shirts and other clothing.

Woven cloth was once important for transport in the days when ships relied entirely on the wind, whether to make war, to trade or simply to travel. Sails were traditionally made of linen, with a little hemp, or cotton, and sail-making was a highly specialised form of cloth weaving, as the weight of the cloth and its strength had to be carefully calculated for maximum efficiency. The quality and weight of a particular weave were crucial – a poor weave could mean poor sail form and a loss of wind power.

Ships' sails, flags and banners, industrial filters, sacks, bags, tents, chair coverings, curtains, woven rugs and knotted carpets – all require woven materials. But there is more to it than practicality. In parts of Africa today and in earlier times in Europe, woven artefacts were also used as a form

of money. Medieval Arab writers describe strips of cloth being used as money in many parts of North Africa, and as recently as the 1950s, in what was then the Belgian Congo, Belgian currency was converted into pieces of cloth before a transaction could take place.

In many parts of the world textiles still represent wealth and status, just as they did in Europe in earlier times when kings and princes would try to acquire as much silk and lace as they could or, in the case of Henry VIII, try to acquire as many tapestries as possible. The king is said to have owned more than two thousand at the time of his death. Tapestries from the great French and Dutch centres of manufacture were sought after for centuries by the rich of Europe. In medieval times, while tapestries were highly valued as indicators of status, they were also very useful at a time when houses were draughty and cold.

ABOVE *A barn-frame loom is constructed from posts and beams. Removable wooden pegs hold it together and ensure that it can be disassenbled and stored when not in use.*

LEFT *The length of cotton fibre, known as staple length, is classified into three groups: fine (30mm/1.2in), medium (26–29mm/1–1.1in) and short (below 26mm/1in).*

{ *In many parts of the world textiles still represent wealth and status* }

THE RAW MATERIALS

The word 'weaving' might instantly conjure up an alliterative image of wool, but many other fibres can be woven and some people are surprised to discover that plant fibres are used to make the vast bulk of the world's fabrics. The two major materials that are processed from plants are cotton and linen.

Cotton

The shrubby Gossipium plants that produce cotton grow in tropical and subtropical

The biggest tapestries might cover all four walls of a room, making it far warmer in winter than it would otherwise have been.

Another sign of wealth and status was lace. Before the fifteenth century lace was made by altering woven fabric, creating a pattern of open holes by removing threads, rather than using braiding and twisting techniques. Today lace is usually made using cotton thread but in earlier times, when it was considered the height of luxury and an important status symbol, lace was made using linen, silk, gold or silver thread.

> *Plant fibres are used to make the vast bulk of the world's fabrics*

And then there is art. From Rembrandt to Pollock, from Bosch to Hockney, much of the great art of recent centuries has been painted on woven canvas. From the fifteenth century onwards canvas gradually replaced wooden panels as the preferred substance for artists to work on, and painterly styles would very likely have been forced down a different path without it.

environments. The part of the plant that is harvested for fibre is the boll, a protective pod formed around the seed that bursts open when the seed is ripe to reveal a fluffy white mass of fibrous cellulose. For most of cotton's history, these bolls had to be picked by hand – hence the infamous use of slaves as cotton pickers in America: the American South built its wealth on slaves and cotton-growing in the nineteenth century.

After picking, which is now done by machines in most countries, the seeds must be removed ('ginning') and the fibre is cleaned, separated ('carded'), stretched ('drawn') and then spun into yarn. The invention of a mechanical cotton gin in 1793 to separate the seeds from the cotton lint set America on the road to becoming a major producer of cheap raw cotton for markets worldwide.

Cotton has been farmed on the Indian subcontinent for some 7,000 years, and today the major cotton-growing countries are China, India, America and Pakistan.

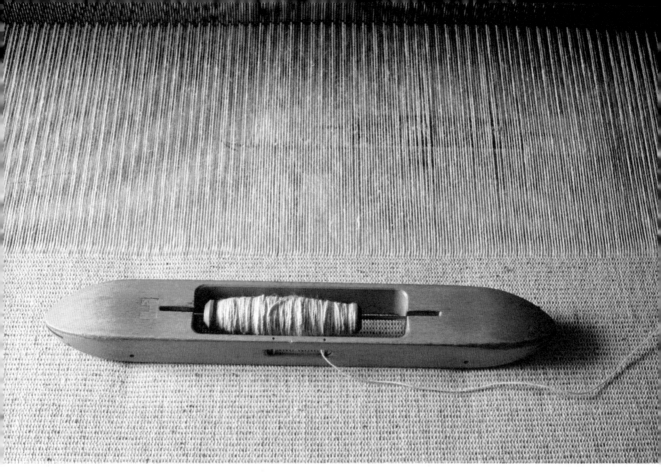

The best and finest cotton, with the longest staple (fibre length), comes from species such as *Gossypium barbadense*, commonly known as Sea Island or Egyptian cotton. American upland cotton (*G. hirsutum*) is a medium staple and less lustrous; while coarse short-staple cotton is used for cheap fabrics.

Linen

The second major plant-based weaving material is linen, made from flax (*Linum usitatissimum*), that wonderful plant whose delicate blue flowers appear for just part of the day, suddenly turning a whole field cerulean. Flax is native to the eastern Mediterranean and Asia, but the best flax has always been grown in western Europe.

Flax is a particularly useful plant: apart from the stem fibres that go to make linen it can be used to make paper, hair gel, medicine, twine and rope and linseed oil.

Flax has been processed to make linen for at least 10,000 years and possibly far longer than that: dyed fibres from a wild flax found in a Georgian cave have been dated to more than 30,000 years ago. The bodies of ancient Egyptian pharaohs were often wrapped in linen, and there is evidence of an Egyptian linen industry 4,000 years ago.

Flax was first introduced into Ireland by the Phoenicians more than 2,000 years ago, but it didn't become an established industry there until about the twelfth century. Ulster became a great centre of flax growing and from the late seventeenth century (when large numbers of Scottish protestants settled in Ulster) linen became a primary industry employing thousands. Flax is still grown in Northern Ireland and the linen produced has enjoyed a resurgence of popularity in recent years for clothing, despite the material's tendency to crease badly.

For the longest fibres, flax is best harvested by hand rather than machine, and preferably pulled rather than cut. The conversion of flax into linen traditionally involved the process of 'retting' – soaking the harvested stems in a pond to loosen the

> *Hessian was used for camouflage material during World War II*

fibres by gentle rotting – followed by beating, 'scutching' (in which the stems are crushed between rollers) and then 'heckling', in which the stems are combed to separate out short fibres and rubbish, leaving the fine long fibres that will be spun into threads for linen.

A coarser fibre than flax, but with similar processing techniques, is industrial hemp, from the plant *Cannabis sativa*, which is woven to make sacking and canvas. It was once more common than flax, especially in rural areas and for military uniforms.

Another plant fibre in this group is jute, the basis of hessian fabric and burlap, made from species in the genus *Corchorus* grown mainly in India and Bangladesh. Again, the processing is similar to that for flax, but jute contains more lignin (woody matter). Like hemp, jute is used for sacking and carpet-backing. For centuries, deep in the holds of ships criss-crossing the world's oceans, hessian sacks were used for the carriage of all kinds of goods. They were ideal for coffee, for example, because they allowed the beans to breathe and prevented rot-inducing condensation. Jute fibres are cheap, easy to weave and very strong, largely because jute has some of the properties of cloth and some of timber. Jute is increasingly popular in India for woven carpets and rugs.

Hessian was also used for camouflage material during World War II (it produces a

ABOVE *The traditional process of grassing simply bleaches the woven linen by natural sunlight.*

LEFT *Linen is the fibre obtained from the flax stalk. Flax combs, or 'brakes', were used in the final step of preparing linen for spinning, removing any straw left in the linen fibre after scutching and hacking.*

wonderfully non-shiny texture), for ghillie suits (landowners loved it because it clothed their ghillies cheaply), and in early times it was the material of choice among religious zealots for making extremely uncomfortable hair shirts! In contrast, jute can also be

use anything else – but far more now comes from Australia and New Zealand.

Wool processing begins with selecting the breed of sheep: different breeds can be broadly divided into those with long lustrous wavy wool, those with short fine wool (downland breeds) and those with strong coarse wool in the uplands; most are white-wooled, but some are noted for their naturally coloured fleeces, much favoured by hand spinners. Next comes shearing the sheep – traditionally by hand, but now with power-driven clippers. There are numerous steps before the wool is ready for weaving, including washing or scouring (traditionally by soaking in diluted urine, or a solution of soda ash) to remove excess natural grease, sorting into grades and staples, untangling the matted fibres, combing or carding the fibre between boards covered originally with prickly teasel heads but later with fine wire

ABOVE *Hand carding is the traditional method of preparing fleece and fibres for spinning by separating and straightening the wool fibres. Hand carders are wooden paddles with teeth, which brush the wool between them until the fibres are aligned in the same direction. Coarse teeth carders are used for wool and mohair, while fine teeth are for cotton and softer fibres.*

RIGHT *Spinning wool transforms a mass of staple fibres into a wool or thread. It can be done by hand, by a spinning wheel, or mechanically.*

converted into imitation silk by selecting its finest threads. In an increasingly green-minded world, jute is finding a new role as an eco-friendly fibre that is woven not only into sacking, burlap and clothing but also into 'geotextiles' – lightly woven fabrics to prevent soil erosion, suppress weeds, protect seedlings and so on.

Wool

Sheep's wool was once the great staple of Europe and particularly England. Much of the wealth of the country was based upon it and it paid for the construction of many a fine medieval church in prosperous wool areas.

Large amounts of wool are still produced in the UK, though many British farmers find that the amount they are paid for their fleeces barely covers the cost of shearing. Top quality wool is still produced in England and many Saville Row tailors still refuse to

hooks, and ultimately spinning the wool into yarn, which might then be dyed in hanks.

Other animals whose fleeces are used by weavers include alpaca and vicuna (native to South America), Angora and cashmere goats, Angora rabbits and even, in some cases, long-haired pet dogs.

Silk

The secret of silk production was discovered by the Chinese at least 5,000 years ago and there was already evidence of a Chinese silk trade to Egypt 3,000 years ago. Ultimately the trade spread to the Indian subcontinent, the Middle East and finally Europe, where the material's arrival must have astonished a population used only to the roughness of wool and linen.

Silk is a fibre comprising animal protein and is produced by a range of insects, including bees, wasps and ants – and of course by spiders to form their webs. But for the textile industry most silk comes from the protective cocoons spun by silkworms – the larvae of a moth, *Bombyx mori*. The larvae eat exclusively one food: the leaves of mulberry trees, and preferably of only one species, the oriental white mulberry (*Morus alba*). The way in which the larvae produce the silk is similar to a spider spinning its web: from two glands they eject a clear proteinaceous fluid, fibroin, through 'spinneret' tubes in the head in long continuous twin filaments that are bound together into a thread by a gummy fluid secreted from different glands. The thread can reach a kilometre (0.6 miles) in length within four or five days, during which time the silkworm winds the silk around itself for protection while it pupates. On silk farms, the silkworms are killed soon after they have spun their cocoons; the cocoons are soaked in hot water or steamed and the thread is reeled out, say eight to twelve cocoons at a time, to form a thread of useful diameter which can then be woven. 'Raw silk' retains the gummy fluid that originally bound the twin filaments and can be 'thrown' to make a weaving yarn by twisting the strands in various ways to form different threads: 'crepe' (for weaving crinkly fabrics), 'tram' (to act as the weft or filling on the loom), 'thrown singles' (for sheer fabrics)

> *Most silk comes from the protective cocoons spun by silkworms*

ABOVE *In Thailand silk threads are still predominantly hand-reeled onto wooden spindles. While machines are occasionally used, only hand reeling can produce three grades of silk: two fine, and one heavier weight.*

Fabric design takes meticulous preparation, calculating precisely where each thread will

RIGHT *It takes a silkworm an average of just 72 hours to spin the prized cocoons, each one made up of 500–1200 silken threads. The cocoons are then heated to prevent the chrysalis encased inside turning into a moth, before bathing them in warm water to bind the silken filaments ready for spinning into thread.*

BELOW *The spinning jenny was operated by turning the driving wheel (which was vertical in later designs) with the right hand, causing the spindles to rotate, while managing the draw bar, which controlled the drafting of the threads, with the left hand.*

James I to introduce silkworm cultivation into Britain in the seenteenth century led to some confusion. A number of old houses in England still have ancient mulberry trees that were planted originally to feed what was hoped to be a domestic silkworm industry. Only too late did those who planted the trees realise that they had planted red mulberry trees instead of white. The red tree produces delicious fruit but is of little use for silkworms.

SPINNING

All of these natural fibres need spinning to convert them into threads that can be used by weavers. The simplest (and most laborious) method of spinning is to twiddle the fibres between your fingers, or roll them on your thigh, teasing out the strands as you do so. An early development was the ancient drop spindle: a slightly tapering stick, several inches long, held vertically with a notch at the top and a circular detachable whorl to weight its other end. It is dangled from an existing thread and the prepared fibre is fed onto the spinning thread from between finger and thumb. The spinning yarn gently tugs and twists the fibres out to join and lengthen the twine. Not easy until you have practised, but you can spin as you walk about. At last, but not until about the fourteenth century in Europe (earlier in Asia), the spinning wheel was introduced, conveniently with a bench to sit on while you spun. It was actually two wheels: a large one driven by a cord attached to a small wheel, itself attached to a horizontal spindle. The spinning wheel was originally turned by

and 'organzine' (for warp threads). The gum can be washed out for a lighter, softer and more lustrous fibre.

Silk became and has remained the luxury material of choice, and China remains by far the largest producer, India being the second largest. Attempts by King

hand, and by about the sixteenth century, by treadle. There were many variations on this basic theme but it all changed dramatically in the 1760s when James Hargreaves invented the hand-powered multi-spool spinning jenny, and Richard Arkwright invented the water frame (powered by water and later by steam), and when Samuel Crompton introduced his spinning mule in 1799. Spinning had become mechanised by the end of the eighteenth century.

HOW WEAVERS WORK

Arguably a great deal of lace making, crocheting and even cross-stitch is weaving of a sort, but when they hear the word weaving most people think of fabric-making on a loom, whether using linen or cotton, silk, wool, or manmade fibres.

> *Spinning had become mechanised by the end of the eighteenth century*

The basic principles of handloom weaving are unchanged in essentials in thousands of years. A wooden frame allows vertical (warp) threads to be stretched down in front of the weaver in parallel with each other. Various methods for keeping the threads in position have been used over the centuries (starting probably with stone weights tied to the ends of each warp thread) but the idea remains the same: the warp threads must be stretched taut and kept parallel with each other.

The weft threads – the ones running horizontally – would originally have been laboriously pulled across and interlaced between the warp threads by hand. Once several lines of thread had been interwoven like this they would be tamped down using a weaver's comb – the teeth of the comb would

be pushed between the warp threads and then pressure exerted downwards to pack the weft threads tightly in place.

Simple looms that rely on weaving the weft threads through the warp threads slowly are still used by traditional Navaho weavers in America, and by weavers in a number of African and Asian cultures. However, more modern looms that allow complex patterns to be created and at a faster pace are now generally used (though by no means exclusively) in the West.

ABOVE *In Navajo weaving, the slit weave technique common in kilims is not used, and the warp is one continuous length of yarn, not extending beyond the weaving as fringe. Iconic motifs and patterns were introduced in the nineteenth century.*

All modern looms use some form of shuttle – that's the device that allows the weft thread to be threaded relatively quickly through the warp. But even with a modern loom the fact that one person is creating the fabric line by line, by hand, means that it is still a slow and highly skilled process.

Before set up the loom must be true and square. The warping process is the first stage of getting the loom ready. It's a complicated business but in essence involves setting up sufficient threads to create the fabric shown in the drawdown – the diagram of the fabric to be woven. The weaver decides how many threads per inch will be required for the design and sets up the appropriate number of spools. A tension box is threaded to ensure an even tension on the threads.

> *The warping process is the first stage of getting the loom ready*

Next, the thread sequence has to be set up to match the pattern, and this has to be perfectly executed to ensure that the fabric works out to plan. The threads are passed through a reed, which controls the density of the warp and a dobby chain (or similar device, according to the type of loom being used) controls the lifting of the harnesses through which the threads have been threaded. It is the lifting of the harnesses as the weaver works that controls the emerging pattern of the fabric. That is an oversimplification of a process that involves a number of intricate parts, but it gives some idea of the complexity of the operation.

Once the warping has been completed the weft thread is wound on bobbins and placed in a shuttle, which in turn sits in what's known as a fly box. When the weaver depresses a foot treadle a complex

For straightforward linen or woollen weaving where there are no complex patterns. Setting up the loom with warp and weft threads is relatively easy, but for more complex patterns – particularly where a number of different colours and types of thread are in use – it can take several days to ensure that all the threads are in position and the loom is correctly set up.

LEFT *The jack loom was created in the early part of the twentieth century for handloom weaving. The shafts work independently, moved by jacks which can be placed on the castle above the shafts, or below.*

FAR LEFT *The simplest 'stick' shuttles have the yarn directly wound on to them. In more complex designs, the yarn is wound on to a 'pirn' that sits within the shuttle.*

mechanical process makes the harnesses lift, creating an opening in the warp called a shed (the gap between the warp threads that allows the weft thread through). Once the shed opens, the shuttle is sent flying across carrying the weft thread through the warp. The weaver then pulls a device known as a beater towards them, and this pushes the weft into place. The weaver then begins the next line.

The process of raising the warp thread to allow the weft thread through is known as shedding. The pick is the name given to the journey of the shuttle across the loom, and taking up the process of winding the new fabric on to a beam.

> *The skills of the handloom weaver can produce fabrics of extraordinary beauty*

Looms

There are a number of different looms, from the ancient simple wooden horizontal frame, through the warp-weighted loom that was in use in ancient Greece and which stands vertically in front of the weaver, to a range of modern looms that retain the handmade craft element while giving the weaver a range of options for creating fabrics.

Perhaps the most basic loom of all is the backstrap loom, where the weaver simply ties the warp threads to a belt on their body at one end and to a tree or post at the other. The weaver's hands are then free to interlace the weft threads while keeping tension on the warp threads by simply leaning back.

Most looms have similar major components: a warp beam, heddles (used to separate the warp threads), harnesses, shuttles (designed to hold the weft thread while weaving is taking place), a reed (a comb-like tool that pushes the weft into place) and take-up roll.

The counterbalance loom has a wooden frame from which shafts hang suspended by pulleys or roller dowels. The shafts move as and when the weaver operates the foot treadles. Counterbalance looms allow the skilful weaver to open a large or small shed according to how hard or how gently the treadles are used. This is an advantage because small sheds tend to produce better selvedges – that is, self-finished edges to the fabric.

The countermarch loom has all the advantages of ease of use associated with counterbalance looms, but also allows the operator to add treadles and shafts (in other words, to increase the capacity of the loom) without the need for a new loom frame. Counterbalance looms come in vertical and horizontal varieties but for all practical purposes weaving is the same on both kinds.

Jack looms are the most popular variety in America and are smaller than counterbalance and countermarch looms. They are also popular with beginners, because they are generally cheaper. With a jack loom, for various reasons to do with the position and action of the shafts, the weaver works with a lower tension, which can lead to skipped threads, poor selvedges and a loose weave. The shafts on this type of loom can also cause the warp threads to break more easily than on other types of loom, because they are constantly under tension from the moment they go into the loom, even when the weaver is not working.

Cloth weaving techniques

Whether for sails, clothes or furnishings, cloth is mostly made on huge industrial looms today, but at the high art end of fabric-making the skills of the handloom weaver can produce fabrics of extraordinary complexity and beauty. These levels of complexity spring from three main weaving methods or types. Plain weave is a straightforward crisscross of warp and weft fibres, and many of the fabrics we use in clothing and furnishing are based on this; basketweave – a variation on plain weave – is a weaving method that involves using

BELOW *Woven fabrics are constructed from two sets of interlacing warp and weft yarns. The warp yarns are usually wound lengthwise on the loom, while the weft yarns interlace the warp at right angles to produce the fabric.*

ABOVE *Different weaves create different properties in a textile beyond pattern, giving the cloth strength or smoothness or allowing it to drape well.*

two or three threads together for each line of warp or weft or both. Twill, a method of weaving that is famously used to make tweed and denim, involves passing the warp thread over one or more weft threads, and then under two or more warp threads. The result is a material that is soft, hangs well and is therefore ideal for clothing. It has a distinct appearance of diagonal lines. Satin weave is a special weave normally used only for silk or polyester and as the name implies it produces woven articles that are silky in appearance and to the touch. To create satin weave, four or more weft threads are carried over a warp thread or, alternatively, four or more weft threads are carried over each

warp thread. Modern computer-controlled jacquard looms can produce these three main weaving styles as well as dozens of other far more complex patterns.

Tapestry weaving

Tapestry weaving – when done by hand – is labour intensive. It is a slow and painstaking process. In earlier times several weavers would have worked side by side with very wide looms for the really big tapestries. It has been estimated that it would take one weaver a month to weave a square metre of a typical late medieval tapestry. The otter and swan hunting tapestry at the Victoria and Albert Museum in London measures 40 sq metres (430 sq foot), so it is easy to estimate the total length of time it would have taken to make it.

The tapestry weavers worked from a cartoon or drawing which was placed under the threads of the loom or behind the weavers, who would turn to consult it every now and then. For the most costly tapestries they used gold and silver thread in addition to coloured wools and silk.

Looms designed to make tapestry are traditionally known as haute lisse and basse lisse looms, but their basic mode of operation is similar to that of fabric looms.

Carpet weaving

Apart from cloth, carpets are perhaps the most important articles that are made on a loom. We still set great store by handmade rather than those produced by machine. Carpets differ from fabric despite having a basic similarity. The similarity is that a warp and a weft are used as the base layer, but the pile is knotted into that base and then trimmed to an even surface. Knotted carpets, made in countless designs from silk and wool and in countries as far afield as Turkey, Pakistan and Persia, have for centuries adorned first our tables and walls and then our floors.

The word 'carpet' comes from the Armenian 'kar', meaning knot or stitch, and the technique for making knotted carpets probably developed originally in the Caucasus and as early as the Bronze Age. By the sixteenth century Persian and other carpets were being widely traded and copied across Europe and Asia. The most important types of knotting in carpet manufacture are the Turkish symmetrical knot and the Persian or asymmetrical knot.

> *The word 'carpet'*
> *comes from the*
> *Armenian 'kar',*
> *meaning knot or stitch*

Cheaper woven carpets or kelims, which also originate in the Middle East, are now made and sold all over the world. Kelims differ from carpets in that they are woven as cloth is woven – there is no pile as there is in a carpet. Kelims have what is called a flat weave, but there are many different types – some so different that they really count as an entirely separate kind of artefact. The soumak, for example, which takes its name from Shemakja in Azerbaijan, is flat woven like a kelim but is also embroidered and has a slightly shaggy appearance as the weft threads serve a decorative and a structural role. Kelims and variations on the kelim are made right across the Near and Middle East, from Turkey to Afghanistan, and their production has changed little over the years – an ancient woven artform that is as popular and useful today as it has been for centuries.

RIGHT *The front and back surfaces are alike in true tapestry, with the exception that where the weaver bridges from one area to another of the same colour, the loose thread is left hanging at the back.*

Organising the yarn into the desired order to make the warp is an exacting process that can take many hours with a complex pattern. Winding onto a warping board, each thread is passed around pegs and back up to cross over itself, this crossing point keeping the threads in the order that they were wound.

I use lots of silk and lycra, for example. Silk doesn't shrink but lycra does, so I created one fabric that involved the lycra actually physically pushing up the silk after the material had been washed to create an effect not unlike bubble wrap! It became one of my best-known fabrics.'

In the great tradition of craftwork, Margo is a firm believer in producing fabric that is both beautiful and useful.

'I do some fabrics so they can simply be hung to be looked at – rather like a painting – but I prefer my fabrics to have a function. If you think about it, so much that surrounds us is woven – clothes, chair covers, carpets, blankets. They might be great to look at but they are also really useful. There is great pleasure in making the everyday practical textiles in our life beautiful so that they can enhance our lives.'

Her interest in the whole world of design is reflected in her collaboration with other artists, designers and crafts people.

'I've collaborated with interior designers for some of my work – creating curtains and chair covers – and I've also worked with fashion designers to create jackets, shoes and other items. It's something I really enjoy but I also like just being in my studio and making scarves and cushions, small purses and lavender bags.'

To ensure that it reaches the widest possible audience, Margo also sells her work at craft fairs and shows and she has collaborated with museums and art galleries on specific projects.

'I've worked with the Tate Gallery and the National Gallery, and with other similar

ABOVE *The warp is made of many threads which make up the backbone of the fabric. These are wound onto the loom at an even tension and then meticulously threaded onto the shafts of the loom. This is done in a specific order so that the patterns and structures can be created.*

complex designs to be woven by hand. But it is essentially much like the kind of looms used a thousand and more years ago.

'It's a one-metre-wide loom and, like all looms, it is complex to set up and operate but it still involves warp and weft, just as an ancient loom would.'

When it comes to designing a fabric, Margo's great passion is colour and texture.

'I'm driven by colour,' she explains, 'but I want the colour and the structure to work together. I create optical patterns of warp and weft that match and complement each other. I create geometric patterns using a technique called 'colour and weave'. 3-D colour surfaces are created with a double cloth fabric. This means that the cloth is made from two layers of fabric which swap over to form patterns and raised surfaces.

institutions in America. A museum will sometimes give me a design idea to tie in with an exhibition, and I develop a fabric that can then be used for all sorts of accessories to be sold in the museum shop.'

Developing a fabric is no easy task. For Margo, it can involve up to five years' work.

'It does take a long time, because my designs are very colourful and complex – I spend hours at my loom coming up with ideas, trying them out and refining them. Once I'm really happy with a fabric its great to work with an industrial mill to put it into production. It's wonderful to see my ideas brought to life in this way.'

Like the weavers of old, Margo is aware that her craft is essentially a slow, meticulous business.

'Working at the loom I can produce perhaps a metre of fabric a day, which isn't much but there is no way to rush it. And on top of that you have to remember that it can take several days just to set the loom up, particularly if I'm using a lot of fine yarn. Set-up time can be as much as five days.'

So how many new designs does Margo produce each year?

'I make ten or twelve new designs each year and it is important for me to keep developing new fabrics. Some of my new designs will become classics – how well they sell is what really determines how long I keep making them.'

The idea that a handloom weaver is behind a design is definitely a selling point in this age of mass production. Apart from anything else, it is a rare skill. Margo reckons that there are fewer than 30 people doing what she does in the UK, and many of these work only part time or they are 'hobby weavers'.

'People don't realise what a slow, painstaking business designing and handloom weaving a fabric is, and that it takes years to learn how to do it. I'm still

ABOVE *The threads are lifted in different combinations creating a shed. The weft yarn is passed using a shuttle.*

BELOW *Before weaving it is important to check the tension of the yarn is even across the loom.*

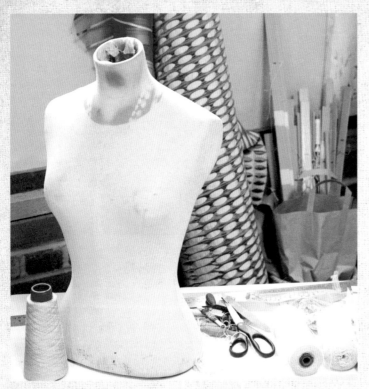

ABOVE *Once the fabrics are woven Margo collaborates with designers of products, interiors and fashion to create a wide range of end uses.*

BELOW *Combining different fibres which shrink and react differently in the finishing creates 3-D fabrics.*

learning even though I've been doing it for years. Once you know how to weave, that's just the start – you have to have an idea in your head of how you can make something look right before you produce it.

'It's a bit like reading music – my designs start as a complex series of crosses on graph paper, but what looks like a mass of marks to most people enables me to visualise the fabric much as a musician can hear the music when they see the notes on paper.'

Margo loves the long tradition of the craft of which she is a part, but she is also fascinated by new materials and how they work with long-established materials.

'I use lots of different fibres because I'm interested in seeing how they react together – I use silk, lycra, cashmere, mohair, lamb's wool, cotton and viscose. My approach is traditional but also modern – what could be more traditional than weaving on a loom by hand? The key point is that I make and design fabrics I love, and hope that others will love them too.'

Most of Margo's designs are geometric but she also uses a Jacquard loom to create a variety of intricate shapes.

{ *I use lots of different fibres because I'm interested in seeing how they react together* }

'I worked with a ceramics company called "People Will Always Need Plates" to create a geometric textile design inspired by Trellick Tower.'

Though weaving was once a big industry in Britain it has declined dramatically, but Margo's enthusiasm and success show that there is a market – and a good one at that – for fabric designed and made carefully, beautifully and by hand.

LEFT **Margo is proud to have combined handweaving technical skills with industrial methods and an entrepreneurial attitude to make weaving and woven fabrics both relevant and accessible in today's society.**

The warp is dressed onto the loom in preparation for weaving, each thread being tied to a separate heddle. The loom's foot pedals operate the shaft which lifts the heddles up and down, allowing the weft yarn to be passed through and create the weave.

The Tradition of Weaving

In the 1920s handloom weaving was closely connected with cottage spinning and dyeing. These three handicrafts had almost become extinct in Britain but were revived in the nineteenth century, despite the easy availability of factory-made woven goods.

Thanks to this revival there were still handloom weavers in Somerset (flax and hemp), Wiltshire (tweed and carpets), Northumberland (wool), the Midlands (ribbon weaving), Kent (wool, hop sacks and rick canvases), Norfolk (linen), the Lake District (wool, silk and linen), Sussex (wool and cotton) and Suffolk (silk), using local plant dyes, local fleeces and local flax crops, just as their ancestors had done for thousands of years and the ancient skills were saved to pass on to the present generation.

We can only speculate how early prehistoric humans may have developed the first woven items. They would have figured out how to twist and lace vines, twigs or reeds into nets for trapping fish (and perhaps they even took their cue from watching birds build their nests), it would have been quite a short step to weaving twig baskets, or weaving rods and plant material to form hut walls and making basic floor mats from interlaced grasses and rushes. And as soon as they had teased out plant fibres and twiddled them together to make longer lengths of twine (the essence of spinning), textile making could begin and fabrics, however crude, could be used for clothing. Given the human instinct for individualism and ornament, it would not be long before those fabrics were being customised with the use of plant dyes to colour the threads and make patterns in the weave. There would also be experiments with other fibres.

But hard evidence of ancient weaving techniques and fabrics is difficult to come by. In Peru relics of simple weaving tools radiocarbon-dated to 5800BCE have been found, and here they were using mainly cotton along the coast, or wool from sheep

and lamoids (llama, alpaca and vicuna are native only to South America) in the mountains. It is thought that they were weaving tapestries and pile carpets.

On the other side of the world, cloth was being woven in Turkey and Mesopotamia (that great commercial centre, trading crossroads and cradle for the development of agriculture) some 10,000 years ago. Woven fabric is perishable and it has been difficult for archaeologists to find early remnants that help in tracking the development of weaving. Traces have survived in environments that are arid, boggy or extremely cold, or if they have been sealed from the elements – especially in tombs.

Egyptian tombs in the Nile Valley, for example, have yielded fragments of

{ *Hard evidence of ancient weaving techniques and fabrics are difficult to come by* }

RIGHT *While fabric remnants are hard to find, information about weaving in history can sometimes be found from other sources. This funerary model, which was carved out of wood, provides valuable information about the looms and tools available at the time, as well as the clothing of that period.*

BELOW *This ancient loom weight, which was found in Aylesbeare Common, Devon, measures 7.5cm (3in) across, and the central hole was chipped out, rather than bored. This artefact provides prehistoric evidence of weaving and loom use.*

woven linen dating back to 5000BCE, and an Egyptian funerary model of a weaver's workshop dated to the nineteenth century BCE, actually shows a horizontal loom being worked by weavers. More specifically, Sumerian clay tablets about 4,000 years old depict a weaving industry.

About 5,000 years ago, Swiss Lake Dwellers were weaving: scraps of woven linen have been found in the bogs, along with whorls for spinning. In Britain, a Neolithic (4000–2500BCE,) pot found in the river Thames in London was imprinted with a woven pattern, and it is thought that the potter created the vessel by lining the inside of a woven basket with wet clay, then heating it to shrink and harden the clay, so that the basket fell away but left its

pattern on the outside of the pot. Weaving as a technique applies to basketry as well as to textiles.

The ancient Hebrews were also weaving 5,000 years ago and their yarns became sophisticated: they were multiple-ply (up to 72-ply) and there are biblical references to gold and silver threads being incorporated into their fabrics. The Hebrews used fine white wool for their best cloth (though priests had to wear pure linen), and for lesser materials they used coloured or black coarse wool and horsehair. The Bible (Deuteronomy, which is thought to have been written in the seventh century BCE) gives detailed information about early Hebrew weaving, including laws that prohibited wearing fabrics made from linen/wool mixtures and others prohibiting married women from spinning in public places or by moonlight.

In China, according to legend, the 'Yellow' Emperor Huang-di (or Huang-Ti), said to be the ancestor of all today's Han Chinese and to have died around 2597BCE, had a mulberry grove in which the trees were suddenly dying. His empress, Hsi-Ling-Shi, discovered little white worms devouring the leaves and spinning their cocoons below the trees. She took some cocoons to her quarters and accidentally dropped one into warm water: it began to unravel and exposed a network of fine fibres. She had discovered silk, and the Chinese quickly became the masters of silk weaving.

The Middle East has played its part in the history of weaving for thousands of years – think Babylonian embroidery and Persian carpets – and a recent archaeological discovery in central Jordan has provided evidence of the area's ancient textile industry. A major find was made within an Iron Age fort at Khirbat Al-Mudaybi, built around 700BCE, on what was then a strategic trade route on the eastern frontier of the ancient state of Moab. Within this fort an excavation team has discovered a quantity of hand-moulded round or cylindrical clay loom weights, each perforated to take multiple threads. So far no evidence of actual looms or other weaving tools have been excavated at this site but archaeologists have good reason to wonder whether woven carpets or tents were being made here some 2,700 years ago.

Loom development

At first, in every part of the world, it would have been simple finger-weaving and web-making, much like basketry and net-knotting, but cultures worldwide developed crude looms at an early stage – and they were broadly similar in those first designs. It is impossible to give time lines on loom development but a broad pattern of development can be described.

A loom is a device that holds the vertical warp threads tightly enough for the weaver to pass the weft threads in and out of them. At its most basic, the spun warp fibres would be suspended from a horizontal tree branch, their loose ends weighted with pebbles or clay weights so that they hung parallel with each other under tension – just such a 'warp-weighted' loom is depicted in the Chiusi Greek vase. The weaver walked from side to side, lifting each warp thread to pass the weft in front of or behind it with the other hand. The cloth developed from the top of the 'loom' – which meant that the weaver needed to push the weft upwards by hand or (with a crude comb) to tighten the weave.

> *It is impossible to give timelines on loom development*

BELOW *Historians believe that textile production was the most commonly practised domestic craft in Roman times. Archaeological excavations have often revealed loom weights such as these, found at the Roman site of Condeixa at Coninmbriga, Portugal.*

The material used for the weights varied according to what was available. Most often special clay weights would be kiln fired for use, or rocks would be chipped or bored. Bags of sand or grit were also used. The required weight varied according to the warp thickness, but the average was about 0.5kg (1lb).

The next step was to use a tapered stick to thread the weft in and out of the warp threads and beat them into place. This big darning-needle stick (darning, for those who can remember how, is weaving at its simplest) would eventually develop into a tapered shuttle, on which the weft threads were wound and then passed between the warp threads. A natural development was to insert a rod behind every other warp thread so that there was a clear passage for the over-sized needle or shuttle to pass above the rod,

without having to lift each warp thread by hand individually.

An adaptation of the warp-weighted loom was the equally primitive horizontal ground loom. Pegs or poles were driven into the ground at equal distances and in two parallel lines spaced several feet apart (according to the length of the finished fabric). The beginning of the warp thread was tied to the outside peg of one row, crossed over to wrap around the corresponding peg in the other row, and back to the second peg in the first row and so on. This system meant that the weaver had to lean over the work to insert the weft and so the next step was to place the horizontal loom over a pit: the weaver could sit comfortably on the edge of the pit.

The more versatile frame loom was a portable structure that could be put up anywhere quickly, without relying on tree branches or driven holes and pits. Four sticks were lashed together to make a right-angled frame. A warp thread was tied to the top stick of this vertical structure, then run down to wrap around the bottom stick, and back up to the top and so on. The

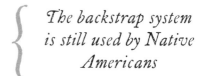

{ *The backstrap system is still used by Native Americans* }

frame could be rested on the weaver's lap, or propped on a table or against a wall.

Even simpler, and just as portable, was the backstrap loom. One end was attached to something solid like a tree trunk; the other was attached to a rod, held in place with a cord around the weaver's waist. The weaver leaned back against the cord to put tension on the warp threads. The weaving could be rolled up at any time and taken to another place to continue the work. The backstrap system is still used by Native Americans in southwestern and Central America.

Backstrap and other simple looms were enhanced by the invention of the slot-and-eye heddle system: the 'eyes' in the middle of these long needle-like devices, made originally of knotted cord but later of wire or flat metal, take the warp threads while loops (or 'doups') at either end of each heddle are threaded to top and bottom cross bars or 'shafts'. The heddles are manipulated to separate the warp threads and allow the weft to pass between them.

But it took a little longer to free up the weaver's hands by adding a foot-treadle and a system of rollers and ropes to the heddle system. The treadle-and-frame loom was first developed in China, during the Shang period (1766–1122BCE). A floor-standing loom with a foot treadle enables the weaver to raise and lower the warp threads at will, hands-free.

All of these early looms are still in use in many parts of the world, and the Chinese treadle-and-frame remains the basis of most modern looms, whether handlooms or industrial ones.

By the medieval period, the draw loom was being widely used. This needed two people to operate it. The weaver did the skilled work but was assisted by a draw boy, who sat on top of the loom frame lifting and lowering the heddles to control the warp as and when required by the weaver. The draw loom could produce far more complex fabrics than were possible in earlier times.

By the late eighteenth century the beginnings of the industrial revolution led to a rapid series of dramatic changes in weaving practice. John Kay's flying shuttle was perhaps the most important of these developments. This flying shuttle (patented in 1733) enabled the weaver to throw the shuttle carrying the weft across the warp threads with just one quick movement and with one hand only. Overnight the speed

ABOVE *In Ecuador it is tradition for the men to be the weavers. The looms are handmade and sanded smooth with glass shards so that the yarn doesn't snag. Ecuadorians traditionally weave with wool because of the country's climate and the material's availability.*

ABOVE *Power looms, such as the Jacquard, seen above in the Macclesfield Silk Museum, were often destroyed by workers, fearful for their employment, when they were first introduced.*

at which cloth could be woven doubled. The flying shuttle is a narrow boat-shaped wooden device that holds a bobbin of thread and it runs in a shuttle race, a narrow shelf along which it glides when pushed, carrying the weft threads rapidly across the loom

The Jacquard loom was invented in 1801 by Joseph Marie Jacquard and is used for creating damask and brocade, for example.

{ *Overnight the speed at which cloth could be woven doubled* }

Rather like a music box or pianola (and, incidentally, exactly like early computers), the loom employs a coded punched-card system to 'tell' it how to weave the fabric. In essence, the punched card runs through the loom and the pattern of holes in it causes the warp threads to move up and down in a pre-determined fashion, thus creating an almost limitless number of patterns of great complexity.

Jacquard looms, even for the hobby weaver, might incorporate several hundred heddles.

In about 1843 the dobby loom appeared, its name a corruption of 'draw boy'. The dobby does the same job as the draw boy (lifting the shafts without the need for treadles) and allows for a greater number of permutations when configuring the shed.

Power looms, as opposed to handlooms, had begun with Edmund Cartwright's loom, invented in 1785. Rapid innovations after that date led to the semi-automatic Lancashire loom of 1841. Further changes to loom design and the invention of James Watt's steam engine as well as the harnessing of water power in the mill districts of North West England meant that, by the mid nineteenth century, vast numbers of looms could be set up and merely watched by a minder. Cloth began to be produced at an increasingly rapid rate, which ultimately brought prices down and made good quality cloth far more widely available.

The ultimate development in the history of weaving has been the computerised loom, by means of which the weaver can enter a threading order and lifting plan into a computer, see what the design will look like and then let the computer instruct the loom about which shafts need to be lifted and when, though the non-industrial weaver still needs to set up and thread the loom by hand and still sits at the loom to insert the weft and beat it into place. It has been said that this development is a natural one: after all, weavers have always dealt in numbers – counting the number of threads, the length and width of the weave, calculating sequence repetitions to create patterns and so on. It made sense to link looms with computers and their use opens up exciting possibilities.

FRAGMENTS FROM THE PAST

Although woven material survives far less often than stone or metal, Britain has a rich legacy of woven and knotted artefacts collected from different parts of the world. These range from fascinating fragments from the ancient Middle East through Roman and medieval fabrics to more recent items. Many of the greatest woven treasures are in National Trust houses up and down the country or in London's Victoria and Albert Museum and the British Museum.

With its hot dry climate, Egypt has provided a number of very early examples of surviving cloth. There is a fragment of linen with a blue and red striped border that dates to around 1550BCE. Apart from its extreme fragility, this remarkable survival looks exactly as a modern piece of linen would look – the basic warp and weft technique simply hasn't changed. It was almost certainly a re-used garment cut up to be used as a mummy wrapping. The blue

dye has been identified as indigo while the red is clearly from madder (an evergreen plant from which red dye was traditionally extracted).

Another very early surviving fragment of cloth is a fourth century Coptic tapestry of multi-coloured wool on linen from Egypt. With its large highly decorated figures of a woman and a man – the man with a pointed hat and the woman carrying a bow – this was probably a wall hanging for someone of wealth and status. The two figures may represent Artemis, the goddess of the hunt, and Actaeon. The borders of this very beautiful hanging are floral with dancing figures interspersed.

From a cave at Mogao, near Dunhuang in China's Gansu province, comes an eighth century Buddhist monastic robe. A large patchwork garment known as a kasaya, it uses beautiful silk patches along a symmetrical vertical axis. There are seven vertical columns of fabric – including purple – with a plain blue border of silk. The border

BELOW *The Lancashire loom was the workhorse of the county's cotton industry. The semi-automatic loom, introduced in 1840, stopped when shuttles needed refilling, but one person could work four looms, thereby quartering the manpower required.*

has printed silk rosettes. Ironically this splendid, richly adorned garment was meant to represent humility!

London's Victoria and Albert Museum is a rich repository for early examples of woven material. It has the world's oldest dated carpet: the Ardabil carpet was completed in 1539/40 and is named after the town of Ardabil in north-west Iran where for three hundred years it lay in the shrine of Shaykh Safi al-Din. The carpet, which is made of knotted wool on pure silk warps and wefts, is 10.5m (34.4ft) by 5m (16.4ft) and is decorated with just one overall design. It has an astonishing 340 knots/sq in (134 knots/sq cm) and would have been woven on a huge loom. The centre of the carpet shows a large yellow medallion surrounded

by a rectangular area that is then filled with intricate fantastical intertwined flowers. The entire pattern includes some ten different colours.

The Bradford Table carpet (all carpets were once made for tables or walls) was made around 1600–1615 from linen and canvas embroidered with silk. It shows an intricate pattern of trees and flowers, and is fruit edged with hunting and countryside scenes.

Woven tapestry work is an important part of the V&A collection. There is a beautifully intricate and detailed woollen and silk tapestry probably once owned by Henry VIII. It is a portrait of Queen Esther, made around 1500 in Brussels. The first workshop in Britain was probably that opened by William

Seldon in Barcheston, Warwickshire around 1570, and the celebrated Mortlake tapestry workshop was established in 1619.

Among the more spectacular survivals are the late medieval tapestries from Hardwick Hall in Derbyshire, which was completed in 1597. Many of its tapestries – particularly in the Great Hall – are still in the house and were listed in an inventory of 1601. The set now in the V&A is also listed in that inventory, but passed to the Dukes of Devonshire and thence to the museum. Known as the Devonshire Hunting tapestries they include Deer Hunt, which was made in the southern Netherlands in about 1440. This woollen tapestry shows the highly ritualistic nature of medieval hunting as well as the magnificent costumes of the participants.

Also made in the southern Netherlands is the Falconry tapestry. This extraordinary work of art, though faded like all the tapestries in the group, reveals a complex interwoven pattern of people, flowers, animals and plants. Other magnificent tapestries in the group include otter and swan hunts, where the costumes of the hunters are so detailed that even the pins in the women's head coverings can be seen.

The best cloth was often kept for important or solemn occasions. A good example is the Brewers Company funeral pall of about 1490, richly worked in cloth of gold and silk velvet with applied embroidery. Another very early rare survival is the Fayrey Family pall, a rich burgundy-coloured velvet in astonishingly good condition considering it was made in the early sixteenth century. It is made from velvet cut pile and cloth of gold, silver gilt, silver and silk embroidery using satin and split stitches.

Early lace collections at the V&A are unrivalled, while National Trust houses across Britain include hundreds of examples

of rare and very beautiful woven material – from the Tudor and earlier embroidered and upholstered chairs and tapestries at Knole in Kent to the Boucher Medallion tapestries at Osterley House in Middlesex.

The British Museum has a fascinating collection of more modern woven artefacts, including a woollen tapestry tunic from early twentieth century Algeria. The tunic was designed to ward off evil spirits but it would also have indicated a person's age, marital status and gender.

London's Fashion and Textile Museum is the ultimate repository for modern textiles. Founded by designer Zandra Rhodes it has a wonderful collection of ultramodern fashion textiles, demonstrating that the art of creative weaving is thriving.

ABOVE Tapestries provided colour, warmth and draught-proofing in bleak fifteenth century rooms with stone walls. The Devonshire Hunting tapestries (Falconry seen above) was accepted by the British Government in the 1430s in lieu of tax payable on the estate of the 10th Duke of Devonshire.

{ *The best cloth was often kept for important or solemn occasions* }

Resources

For those who are interested in finding out more about the crafts in this book, this section gives some suggestions for organisations, training opportunities and collections.

GENERAL INFORMATION

The **Art Guide** (www.artguide.org) gives a lengthy list of museums and collections, categorised by the type of craft, with web links to the appropriate site.

Crafts in the Countryside (www.craftsintheenglishcountryside. org.uk) offers an invaluable text (full-length book) that can be downloaded as pdf files, published in 2004 by the **Countryside Agency** and stuffed with reports and practical information on a wide range of crafts, including blacksmithing, farriery, saddle and harness making, wheelwrighting, pole lathe turning and other greenwood crafts, basketry and chair seating, millwrighting, and heritage building restoration crafts (flint work, dry stone walling, brickwork restoration, timber framing, stonework and thatching). The (late-lamented) Countryside Agency also ran a New Entrants Training Scheme (NETS) that covered crafts such as forgework, furniture making, thatching, wheelwrighting, wood machining, blacksmithing and farriery.

The **UK Craft** website directory (www.ukcraftwebsites.co.uk) gives details for a range of crafts, including those working in glass, wood, stone and textiles.

The **Building Conservation** website (www.buildingconservation.com) offers a comprehensive directory of organisations that might be of interest to those whose crafts are relevant, as well as directories of companies, products and services.

In days gone by, there were numerous **craft guilds** and City of London 'Worshipful Companies' or livery companies representing and controlling many of the traditional crafts, going back in some cases to medieval times. Today, there are still more than a hundred City of London guilds but many have lost their major role and influence. Some are simply ceremonial or charitable organisations that may, or may not, be able to provide funds in support of the craft or may have barely any connection at all with the craft in their name. In theory they are all now philanthropic fellowships and, whether firmly bound or loosely tied to a craft or trade, they usually support education, research and welfare or nurture the skills of those actively involved in the craft. The more active ones do all they can to support craftsmen and often to develop training opportunities. Those for the blacksmiths, goldsmiths,

weavers, furniture makers, wheelwrights, carpenters and stone masons are among the most active and are noted for each chapter below. These chapter sections also list other potentially useful organisations.

TRAINING

Some local technical and art/design colleges offer appropriate courses, and various museums offer workshops.

City & Guilds (www.city-and-guilds.co.uk) gives a wide range of vocational qualifications, including in sectors such as textiles, glass, metal and wood. The **City & Guilds of London Art School** (www.cityandguildsartschool.ac.uk) offers courses in, for example, architectural stone carving, ornamental wood carving, gilding and letter-carving, sculpture and conservation studies.

The **Crafts Council** (www.craftscouncil.org.uk) is a useful starting point for craft courses. There are numerous county-based **Rural Skills centres** and trusts that offer courses. For example, **Devon Rural Skills Trust** (www.devonruralskillstrust.co.uk) for stone facing, cobble-stoning, basketry, greenwood crafts; or **Dorset Centre for Rural Skills** (www.dorseturalskills.co.uk) for blacksmithing, stone letter carving, glassblowing, greenwood crafts and sustainable building; or **Halifax Creative & Conservation Skills Centre** (www.halifaxcreative.org, 01422 399330) at Calderdale College for masterclasses in, for example, stone carving. County **Wildlife Trusts** often offer courses in greenwood crafts, blacksmithing and metalwork.

English Heritage (www.english-heritage.org) can direct you to training in heritage skills, as can the **National Trust** (www.nationaltrust.org.uk). Both bodies are involved, along with the **National Heritage Training Group** (www.nhtg.org.uk), in the **Heritage Lottery Fund's traditional building craft skills bursary scheme** (www.buildingbursaries.org.uk), which offers training in blacksmithing, brick masonry, carpentry and joinery, flint working, ironwork, stone conservation, roofing, wheelwrighting and other construction crafts. The government is establishing employer-led centres of excellence as part of the **National Skills Academy** (www.dius.gov.uk/skills/sector_skills_council/nsa) that might have courses of interest to craftworkers.

The **Herefordshire College of Technology** (www.hct.ac.uk, 0800 032 1986) has a Centre for Rural Crafts and their courses include blacksmithing, farriery, metalwork and welding, construction, furniture making, wheelwrighting and thatching. Many technology, art/design and other colleges offer craft courses.

The **Building Crafts College**, Kennard Road, Stratford, London E15

1AH (www.thebcc.ac.uk, 020 8522 1705) offers courses on fine woodwork, carpentry and joinery, stonemasonry and historic building conservation, while **Lambeth College**, Vauxhall Centre, Wandsworth Road, London SW8 2JY (www.lambethcollege.ac.uk, 020 7501 5010) has a range of building courses, including stonemasonry.

The **London Metropolitan University** (www.londonmet.ac.uk) offers short courses in the Sir John Cass Department of Art, Media and Design that include silversmithing and jewellery, and furniture making

West Dean College, near Chichester in West Sussex (www.westdean.org.uk, 01243 811301) has a wide range of arts/crafts courses including stone sculpture, figure carving, letter carving, walling, building conservation.

The **West Wales School of the Arts** (www.wwsota.ac.uk, 01554 748204) has a sculpture degree course in stone carving, metal construction, bronze casting and mould making.

Several large old country houses and the like offer courses and hands-on experience in building conservation work. For example, the **Woodchester Mansion Trust** (www.woodchestermansion.org.uk, 01453 861541) has master classes in stone vaulting, window glass, stone slating repairs and traditional skills such as lime mortar and lime plaster work.

Open-air and heritage museums that offer a range of craft courses:

Chiltern Open Air Museum: www.coam.org.uk (01494 871117) (pole lathe, rag rug, basketry,

blacksmithing, flint, vernacular building skills etc).

Dean Heritage Centre: www.deanheritagemuseum.com (01594 822170) (pole lathe, also visits to Whitecliff Ironworks).

Rural Life Museums Action Group: www.ruralmuseumsnetwork.org.uk (lists rural life museums by area).

Weald and Downland Open Air Museum: www.wealddown.co.uk (large number of courses in all sectors covered by this book).

MUSEUMS

The most comprehensive and largest collections for all the crafts in this book are at the two big London museums, the British Museum and the Victoria and Albert Museum:

British Museum: www.thebritishmuseum.ac.uk (020 7636 1555)

Victoria and Albert Museum: www.vam.ac.uk/collections/ (020 79422000)

Other general museums of interest:

Beamish Museum: www.beamish.org.uk

Museum of English Rural Life: www.reading.ac.uk/merl (extensive archives on rural crafts and industries, and object collections).

Museum of Lakeland Life and Industry: www.lakelandmuseum.org (01539 722464).

Petrie Museum of Egyptian Archaeology: 020 7679 2884 (part of University College London with

Egyptian/Sudanese archaeological artefacts including linen 5000BCE, monumental sculpture 3000BCE, earliest examples of metal, worked iron beads, glazing, costumes back to 2400BCE, faience, tools and weapons, stone vessels, jewellery).

National Museum Wales (Amgueddfa Cymru): www.museumwales.ac.uk/en/rhagor (this website gives details of the national collections in the various Welsh museums, including the national wool, slate, coal and waterfront museums).

Brooking Collection: www.dartfordarchive.org.uk/technology/art_brooking

WOODCRAFT

Organisations:

The Carpenters Company (Worshipful Company of Carpenters): www.thecarpenterscompany.co.uk

The Furniture Makers Company (Worshipful Company of Furniture Makers): www.furnituremkrs.co.uk (020 7256 5558).

Association of Pole Lathe Turners: www.bodgers.org.uk

British Woodworking Federation: www.bwf.org.uk (0870 458 6939).

Institute of Carpenters: www.instituteofcarpenters.com (020 7256 2700) (membership open to carpenters, furniture and cabinet makers, boat builders, joiners, shopfitters, structural post and beam carpenters, heavy wheelwrights, wood carvers and wood turners).

Wooden Boatbuilders' Trade Association: www.wbta.co.uk

Training:

Green Wood Trust: www.greenwoodcentre.org.uk

Small Woods Association: www.SmallWoods.org.uk

Living Woods Assistantships: www.living-wood.co.uk

Bill Hogarth Apprenticeship Trust Scheme: www.coppiceapprentice.org.uk

Collections:

Wycombe Local History and Chair Museum: www.wycombe.gov.uk/museum (01494 421895).

THATCHING

Organisations:

National Council of Master Thatchers Association: www.ncmta.co.uk (list of county master thatchers associations).

National Society of Master Thatchers: www.nsmtltd.co.uk (01844 281208) (lists of individual master thatchers by region).

British Reed Growers Association: www.brga.org.uk

Broads Reeds and Sedgecutters Association: www.reedcutters.norfolkbroads.com

North Norfolk Reed Cutters Association: www.norfolkreed.co.uk

Thatching Advisory Services: www.thatchingadvisoryservices.co.uk

Conservation of Historic Thatch Committee: www.historicthatch.org (01460 240027).

STONEMASONRY

Organisations:

The Masons Company (Worshipful Company of Masons):

www.masonslivery.co.uk

English Stone: www.englishstone.co.uk

National Association of Monumental Masons: www.namm.org.uk

Stone Federation of Great Britain: www.stone-federationgb.org.uk

Training:

City of Bath College: www.citybathcoll.ac.uk (01225 312191).

Edinburgh's Telford College: www.ed-coll.ac.uk (0131 332 2491).

Moulton College: www.moulton.ac.uk (01604 4911310).

Orton Trust: www.ortontrust.org.uk (01536 711600) (restoration and monumental carving on redundant church near Kettering).

Weymouth College: www.weymouth.ac.uk (01305 764744) (stonemasonry, stone carving, letter cutting and stone restoration work).

York College of Further and Higher Education: www.yorkcollege.ac.uk (01904 770400)

METALWORKING

Organisations:

Worshipful Company of Blacksmiths: www.blacksmithscompany.org.uk

Worshipful Company of Farriers: www.wcf.org.uk (01923 260747)

Worshipful Company of Goldsmiths: www.thegoldsmiths.co.uk

Worshipful Company of Tin Plate Workers: www.tinplateworkers.co.uk

British Artist Blacksmiths Association (BABA): www.baba.org.uk (01526 830303)

National Association of Farriers, Blacksmiths and Agricultural Engineers: www.nafbae.org (02476 696595) (journal: www.forgemagazine.co.uk, 01332 843107).

Blacksmiths Guild (incorporating the Guild of Wrought Ironwork Craftsmen of Wessex and the Blacksmith and Metalworkers Association of South West): www.blacksmithsguild.co.uk (01626 890503).

Farriery Training Agency: www.farrierytraining.co.uk (01733 319770).

Training:

Cold Hanworth Forge and Blacksmithing School: www.teachblacksmithing.com (01673 866700).

Farriery Training Agency/Service: www.farrierytraining.co.uk (01733 319770).

London Metropolitan University: www.londonmet.ac.uk (courses in silversmithing and metalwork)

Collections:

Ironbridge museums: www.ironbridge.org.uk for details of ten local museums in this World Heritage Site, including Colebrookdale Museum of Iron, Museum of the Gorge, Jackfield Tile Museum, Coalport China Museum and Abraham Darby's classic Iron Bridge.

Whitecliff Ironworks via Dean Heritage Museum: www.deanheritagemuseum.com

GLASSMAKING

Organisations:

British Glass: www.britglass.org.uk

British Lampwork Company: www.britishlampwork.co.uk

British Society of Master Glass Painters: www.bsmgp.org.uk (01643 862807).

British Society of Scientific Glassblowers: www.bssg.co.uk

Glass Association: www.glassassociation.org.uk (includes links to numerous glass-related websites – museums, organisations, clubs, resources etc).

Guild of Glass Engravers: www.gge.org.uk (0208 446 4050) (includes list of courses at various colleges).

International Festival of Glass: www.ifg.org.uk

International Guild of Glass Artists: www.igaa.org (in USA)

International Society of Glass Beadmakers: www.isgb.org (in USA)

National Glass Centre: www.nationalglasscentre.com (0191 515 5555).

Church Stained Glass Window Database: www.stainedglassrecords.org

Training:

Glass Making Online: www.glassmakingonline.com (techniques, videos, history)

Collections:

Corning Museum of Stained Glass (New York): www.cmog.org (the world's largest collection).

Stained Glass Museum, Ely: www.stainedglassmuseum.com (01353 660347) (also workshops in glass painting, glazing, fusing etc).

World of Glass, St Helens: www.worldofglass.com (08700 114466) (live glassblowing demonstrations, history of glass, Victorian glass furnace).

WEAVING

Organisations:

Worshipful Company of Clothworkers: www.clothworkers.co.uk

Worshipful Company of Weavers: www.weavers.org.uk (020 7606 1155)

Association of Guilds of Weavers, Spinners and Dyers: www.wsd.org.uk (gives contact details for local guilds). See also: www.onlineguildwsd.org

Interweave: www.interweave.com (useful site for weaving terminology)

Training:

Coldharbour Mill Working Wool Museum, Uffculme: www.coldharabourmill.org.uk (01884 840960)

Online Guild: www.onlineguildwsd.org

Collections:

American Museum in Bath: www.americanmuseum.org (01225 460503)

National Wool Museum (Amgueddfa Wlân Cymru): www.museumwales.ac.uk/en/wool (processing from fleece to fabric, historic machinery in Cambrian Mills, textile gallery).

CRAFTERS FEATURED IN THE BOOK

Andy Oldfield: www.thefringeworkshop.co.uk

Matt Williams, David Bragg: www.rumpelstiltskin-thatching.co.uk

Guy Mallinson: www.mallinson.co.uk

Sophie Lister Hussain: www.lightlust.co.uk

Don Barker: www.theblacksmiths.co.uk

Margo Selby: www.margoselby.com

Index

ACKNOWLEDGEMENTS

Thanks to all those craftsmen and women who gave up their time to explain things to me, and to Paul Felix, Verity Muir, Emily Pitcher and Neil Baber. Thanks also to Charlotte, Emma, Katy, James, Alex and Joe.

I'd like to say a special thank you to Val Porter who brilliantly edited each chapter of what is, by any standards, a complex and detailed book. Val's sterling efforts helped turn what might have been a sow's ear into what is undoubtedly a silk purse!

Thanks also to Monty Don and the Ricochet production team; the mastercrafters Matt Williams, David Bragg, Guy Mallinson, Sophie Hussain, Margo Selby, Don Barker and Andy Oldfield; and to Caroline Swash, Harvey Edington, Julian Alexander and Alexandra Henderson.

PICTURE CREDITS